LEARNING THEORIES AND THE DESIGN OF E-LEARNING ENVIRONMENTS

Bijan B. Gillani

University Press of America,® Inc.
Lanham · Boulder · New York · Toronto · Oxford

Library of Congress Cataloging-in-Publication Data

Gillani, Bijan B.
Learning theories and the design of e-learning environments /
Bijan B. Gillani.
p.   cm
Includes bibliographical references (p.) and index.
1. Internet in education. 2. Web sites—Design.
3. Learning, Psychology of. I. Title.

LB1044.87.G47 2003
371.33'467'8—dc21   2003055994 CIP

ISBN 0-7618-2604-1 (paperback : alk. ppr.)

Dedicated to my wife whose devotion to her family is unparalleled.

Table of Contents

Preface

The dramatic advances in the power of personal computers and the explosive growth of the Internet in recent years have revolutionized the way students and teachers view technology in education. These technical advances have made it possible to produce educational materials and transmit them over the Web. In parallel to these technological advances, the fields of educational psychology and interface design have made phenomenal contributions to curriculum planning and visual design, respectively. A synergy of these three fields would enable instructional designers to produce effective electronic educational materials, which has become known as e-learning. E-learning in its strictest sense covers training, teaching, and learning programs that use networked technologies as the medium of choice to deliver instruction.

Unfortunately, a great majority of e-learning sites lack any theoretical foundations for content organization and interface design. These sites, all designed by highly intelligent and well-intentioned educators, appear to be the result of an urgency to be on the Web. Such a rush to be on the Web has resulted in the importation of instructional text-based materials onto the Web without careful planning or consideration of the theoretical foundations for instructional design.

There is a fundamental need for a pedagogical approach to designing e-learning environments whose foundations are supported by a theoretical framework for effective content organization and practical interface design. The rationale for this textbook is to introduce educators and e-learning designers to pedagogical models that provide the framework for effective content organization for curriculum as well as visual design principles that support development of interactive learning environments.

To give the reader a sense of the organization, the book begins with an introductory chapter with two purposes. First, it introduces the reader to new challenges facing education in the twenty-first century. Second, the introduction sets the tone and the organization for the remainder of the book, which is divided into three parts.

Part I deals with the learning theories and teaching models that educators need to know in order to determine the structure and content organization of e-learning environments. It includes four chapters. Chapter two discusses behavioral theories and structured teaching models that can be applied to interactive e-learning environments. Chapter three deals with cognitive theories and constructive e-learning environments. Chapter four is concerned with social theories and collaborative activities that can be applied to a social inquiry-teaching model for the Web. Chapter five focuses on psychological theories and how such an approach assists in the design of thematic e-learning environments. To illustrate how these different learning theories and teaching models can be applied, all examples in this part are selected and illustrated from NASA's Web sites that were designed for educators.

Part II is concerned with educational interface design. It includes four chapters. Chapter six is concerned with the foundations of interface design. This chapter opens up with a definition and the process of educational interface design. It continues with an overview of human perceptual theories and design techniques. Finally, the chapter concludes with some preliminary guidelines for interface design. In chapter seven you will learn about visual interfaces. There will be detailed discussion and examples of visual design elements such as icons, menus, typography, colors, and others. Chapter eight is further discussion of visual design elements such as animation, video, and audio. Chapter eight also provides an introduction to Macromedia Flash MX, as the authoring tool of choice, whose features support incorporation of animation, sound, and video for e-learning. Finally, the purpose of Chapter nine is to discuss how to plan and develop a simple and elegant page layout, and how to create effective site architecture for e-learning.

Part III of the book is concerned with a systematic design process. This part includes one chapter. Chapter ten focuses on the process of e-learning design that includes planning, design, production and maintenance.

Bijan B. Gillani
March 2003

Acknowledgment

Completing a writing project on e-learning is a group effort that cannot be achieved without contributions from others. There were numerous people who have supported me in completing this book. Four groups of people made sustained contributions.

First, friends and family that emotionally and intellectually supported the arduous task of completing this book. I am especially thankful to my wife Judy A. Gillani. She was the source of inspiration, persistence, and stability. She also served as an editor during the time that I was involved in writing this book. I am also thankful to my daughter, my brothers, and my parents who were the sources of constant encouragement.

Second, I would like to express my gratitude to the educational technology staff at NASA who has contributed to the content of this book. In particular, I would also like to acknowledge the contributions of Ms. Susan Ashby, Ms. Christina O'Guinn, and Dr. Thomas Pinelli and Ms. Shannon Ricles for offering their expertise and insight into completing chapters two, three, and five respectively.

Third, I would like to thank my colleagues at the California State University for making wonderful suggestions. In particular I would like to thank the editorial comments that were made by Dr. Steve Borish. I am also thankful to Dr. David Stronck for providing editorial suggestions.

Finally, there were countless students in the graduate program in Educational Technology at the California State University who added their ideas, their teaching experience, and their insights toward completion of this book. Without fantastic contributions from these groups, this book could not have been completed.

Chapter 1
New Challenges

Telling is not teaching: listening is not learning, Anonymous

To solve the problem of homeless people, a popular mayor of a metropolitan center took the initiative of banning a tent city for the homeless in a rich and powerful district. The homeless people just moved to a less powerful district in the city. The solution proposed by the mayor became the problem for the new district. The mayor became more popular in the more affluent district and was reelected for another term. In order to truly solve the homeless problem, the mayor needed to propose solutions that would meet the new challenges of modern society rather than just shifting the problem.

Unfortunately, we do the same thing in education. Education is, by its very nature, a dynamic and evolving process and is susceptible to adaptation to the demands of the environment and to new challenges. Rather than facing the new challenges modern society demands of its educational systems, we constantly shift the problems, provide temporary solutions, or offer remedial programs. In most situations, the solutions become new problems in other aspects of the educational process. For example, reducing the number of students per classroom by placing less qualified teachers in the classroom is not a remedy. Or purchasing computers for schools at a huge cost without much attention to providing training for teachers as to how to integrate the new technology into their curriculum is another example of temporary solutions that have proven to be ineffective.

The reality is that the goals of education for the twenty-first century are drastically different from the educational standards that were set a century ago. Rather than focusing our attention on the new challenges society demands for the twenty-first century, we try to remedy an outdated educational system by shifting its problems from one area to another.

The present practice of a telling-and-listening approach in our schools stems from standards that were set at the beginning of the twentieth century. The influx of immigrants at that time forced the educational system to adapt the scientific method of organizing factories to structuring schools. The goals of the scientific method were efficiency, measurement, and mass production. The same goals for factories and assembly lines were adopted for schools.

To reach their goals, school administrations encouraged the design of curriculum, instruction, and assessment based on a factory model (Apple, 1990). Students were regarded as raw material. Teachers were workers whose job was to alter the raw material (students) into a useful commodity in the most efficient and measurable manner. Instruction was based on breaking down educational content materials into smaller manageable chunks. These bits and pieces of information were taught to students to fill the perceived blank slates of their mind. Students were assessed on rote memorization of these bits and pieces. If they passed, students were moved into the next level of the assembly line. If not, then they had to learn the information till the assessment determined that they were capable of moving into the next level of the assembly. In such an efficient and factory oriented fashion, it was assumed that when students finished school (the end of the assembly line), they would graduate to be functional and responsible commodities for society.

The factory-oriented approach was efficient and achieved its goals. It was a solution to the needs of the society at the turn of the twentieth century. Today, we often hear the claim that our schools are getting worse. Unfortunately, we generally attribute our schools failure to lack of student effort, the incompetence of teachers, or parental indifference. We try to solve the problems by piecemeal remedial reforms that shift them from one section to another. What we, like the mayor, fail to take into consideration is that yesterday's solution to the societal needs of the twentieth century has become the unsolved educational problem of the twenty-first century.

Today, our society, business communities, scientific institutions, industry, and international forces have different expectations and new challenges that were not present at the turn of the twentieth-century. The notion of individualism and a Marlboro Man mentality has been replaced by the belief in collaboration, inquiry methods, and the need for an interdisciplinary approach to solve social, business, scientific, industry, and international problems. These paradigm shifts, which reflect today's societal expectations and challenges, are due to four fundamental developments that have rocked the foundations of education in recent years. These developments are information overload, student diversity, new learning theories, and the explosion of the Web as a medium of instructional delivery. These four parameters provide a challenge to education that will significantly alter the educational process and will transform it from a factory model to a student-centered model in the years to come. As the first step to breaking away from traditional education and pondering upon new standards for the twenty-first century, let us briefly look at these parameters.

Information Overload

Traditional education never considered the concept that humankind has the ability to create more information than individuals can absorb. Information was viewed to have limits and anyone, given enough time, could absorb all information within a field. Contrary to this conception, today information overload has become an ordinary occurrence.

A common anxiety I often perceive in the behavior of my graduate students is that they never have adequate time to learn what they need to know. I generally do not admit to it, but I suffer from the same type of anxiety. I spend twice as much time to prepare for my classes as ten years ago. The fundamental reason for such devotion, in addition to my love of teaching, is due to the ever-increasing amount of information that I need to feel adequately prepared for my lectures.

I am not the first to be confronted with information anxiety. The phrase *information overload* was first popularized by Alvin Toffler (1970). Furthermore, Saul Wurman (1989) expanded upon Toffler's concept by explaining that information overload leads to *information anxiety*. What is interesting is that the explosion of information is not a haphazard phenomenon. It is growing and following a specific pattern. James B. Appleberry (1992) has provided a systematic explanation of information growth:

> The sum total of humankind's knowledge doubled from 1750-1900. It doubled again from 1900-1950. Again from 1960-65. It has been estimated that the sum total of humankind's knowledge has doubled at least every five years since then... It has been further projected that by the year 2020, knowledge will double every 73 days.

In the past, students could get away with memorizing a set of static facts and figures. Our society functioned on a slower pace to change: what we learned in school was sufficient to satisfy the demands of the time. Today, however, change is not only a central fact of life, but its pace has accelerated into an inaccessible level. If students are having information anxiety today, what shall we do when information is doubling every 73 days in the year 2020? One rational answer is to train students to learn how to learn in an ever-changing society. In order to develop such a training model, we need to adopt a student-centered curriculum where students can become adept to collaborate, find, analyze, organize, evaluate, and internalize new information in light of their own needs based on their academic and cultural backgrounds. Rather than forcing students to grapple with information explosion, student-centered curriculum focuses on personalized content that is limited to the students' needs.

Student Diversity

The second parameter that challenges the educational system today is that the social composition of our students has changed drastically from a traditional homogeneous group to heterogeneous diverse groups. Not too long ago, it was assumed that students in our schools had essentially the same linguistic, cultural, and academic backgrounds. The truth of the matter is that there has always been considerable linguistic, cultural, and academic diversity in American schools, even though it was never sufficiently appreciated by the dominant mainstream culture. Not long ago, it was acceptable to assume that diversity among the student population was an exception and limited to academic levels. Students were considered to have a single cognitive capacity, which was often evaluated based on their IQ scores without much consideration given to their other personal attributes. The slow learners were placed in special schools or classes. The others attended traditional classes where one curriculum was adequate to deal with linguistically and culturally homogeneous groups of students.

The concept of a single cognitive capacity to define human intelligence was originally designed by Alfred Binet (1911) for mentally challenged children. Later, it became known as the Intelligence Quotient, or IQ test. The IQ test has come to be a standard test in the U.S. for measuring the raw intelligence of students. Advocates of using the IQ test push for cost-effective assessment in the form of multiple choice and fill the bubble exams. The result is that every student gets the same instructional model regardless of his or her learning styles.

Howard Gardener (1983) challenged the commonly held belief of a uniform cognitive capacity for all humans by hypothesizing that human beings are capable of at least seven basic intelligences. In his book *Frames of Mind* (Gardner, 1983), Dr. Gardner seriously questioned the validity of determining children's single intelligence away from a natural setting. Instead he proposed that intelligence has more to do with multiple cognitive capacities. Based on his extensive research, Gardner (1983) then divided human intelligence into seven distinct yet related categories that included the linguistic, logical-mathematics, spatial, bodily-kinesthetic, musical, interpersonal, and intrapersonal intelligences. In 1996 he added one additional intelligence, which he called Naturalist Intelligence, to his original seven categories.

Partly because of Gardner's influence and partly because of societal changes, today the American educational system has accepted that diversity among students is no longer an exception in our schools, but a norm. The concept of one curriculum for all is no longer acceptable or applicable in schools. Today's schools are composed of minority, immigrant, honor, bright, passive, physically challenged, exceptional, and academically challenged students. It would be a mistake to apply the traditional approach of one textbook, one curriculum to such diverse groups of students with their own special social characteristics, communication styles, personality, cognitive ability, linguistic style, and academic backgrounds. Such diversity challenges educational standards for the twenty-first century and demands a paradigm shift toward the need for student-centered design.

Learning Theories

During the last four decades, research has generated new information about the human brain and the learning process that seriously challenges the traditional practice and drill approach to education. Researchers (e.g. Posner, M. and Marcus Raichle, 1994) support the concept that the brain is a pattern-seeking device that analyzes specific features from the environment and then generates permanent neural activities that represent these features. These newly formed neural patterns are not occurring at random. Rather, they are being combined and organized with prior knowledge according to core concepts or major themes that guide the thinking, memory, and problem solving of students. Meaningful learning occurs when human memory is formed based on the organization of incoming patterns. In such a dynamic process, the social environment plays a major role in influencing the human brain's pattern seeking capabilities. Research (Bransford, et al, 1999, Piaget, 1952) on the human brain also reveals that:

- Learning changes the physical structure of the brain.
- Structural changes alter the functional organization of the brain.
- Learning organizes and reorganizes the structure of the brain.

• There are critical periods of brain development.

Research on the human brain and human learning (Bransford, et al, 1999) is shattering old concepts of teaching and learning. According to this research, there are five different themes that have changed the conception of learning in recent years:

1. Memory and structure of knowledge: O'Keefe and Nadal (1978) discovered two types of memory: *taxon* and *locale*. Taxon memory is concerned with facts and figures and depends on rehearsal and rote memorization. This type of memory is like memorizing the capitals of countries, basic skills in mathematics, and chemical symbols. Because it is non-contextual and not integrated with prior knowledge, the retrieval of this type of memory is difficult when it is needed for problem solving. The locale memory is a natural memory that is biologically driven by the limbic system. According to O'Keefe and Nadal, locale memory is contextual and situational based. The hippocampus in our limbic system creates a spatial and contextual map of the environmental input. These maps are continuously reconstructed in our memory as the new information is combined with prior information. Therefore, our memory becomes internal and virtually permanent.

2. Analysis of problem solving and reasoning: Experts are those individuals who have organized their taxon memory into their locale memory according to the big picture of some core concepts. A novice, on the other hand, simply memorizes new information and attempts to encode it into long-term memory without much regard to its organization. The difference between the ways an expert learns to organize information and the novice who just memorizes new information becomes apparent when it comes to retrieval and problem solving. The former can easily retrieve relevant information to solve the problem at hand, whereas the novice attempts in vain to use a variety of approaches to solve the problem at hand. In other words, experts have achieved meaningful knowledge structures and problem solving abilities and novices have not.

3. Early foundations: Children are born with a biological predisposition to learn. They may lack experience, but they have the ability to reason and to solve problems. As the result of their biological predisposition to learn, to solve problems, and their personal interaction with the world, children enter formal education with their own backgrounds. Misinterpretation of these backgrounds by educators will interfere with the process of learning.

4. Metacognition processes and self-regulatory capabilities: Metacognition refers to the knowledge about oneself as a learner (Flavell, 1976). Learners can be taught strategies to monitor and regulate their own learning. These strategies include planning, monitoring, and regulating. These strategies are important in helping students learn how to learn.

5. Cultural experiences and community participation: Researchers (e.g. Vygotsky 1978, 1992, Bronfenbrenner, 1989) have argued that a child's development cannot be understood by a study of the individual. One must also examine the external, social, and historical world in which the individual's life develops. Development is a collaborative enterprise between the members of the society and the child. Each member of the society assists the child by providing a learning environment that enables the child's cognitive development. This learning assistance is repeated many times during ontogenetic development and enables the child to master the cognitive, linguistic and cultural patterns of his or her environment.

Based on the results of research on the human brain and how people learn, new models of teaching have been developed that help students become better learners. There are numerous teaching models available to educators today (see Gillani, 1994, Bruce, 1992). These teaching models can be used for different types of learning and different types of learners. Depriving our students of the findings of new research on the human brain and models of teaching by oversimplifying teaching and asking them to follow one curriculum for all severely restricts the natural learning ability of our students. We need to pay attention to curriculum design and instructional models that are student-centered and are based on the findings of learning theories and models of teaching.

Web as a Medium of Instructional Delivery

The last parameter that has challenged our educational system is the explosion of the Web as an instructional delivery medium. The Web is a reform tool that enables educators to create educational settings promoting meaningful learning. Unfortunately, most educational Web sites today do little more than present text-based educational content dressed up with a few graphics and in some cases animation. These traditional educational approaches, dressed up in a new medium of delivery, do not use the full potential of the Web. The Web is much more than a mere presentation tool.

The Web, as an educational reform tool, is a flexible multimedia communication network that can combine content presentation, interactive communication for collaboration, and research for further learning to be a production tool for students' hands-on activities. These four features of the Web (presentation, communication, research, and production) place educators in a unique position to become architects of educational settings that would satisfy the demands of the new educational challenges for the 21st century.

The first feature of the Web is content presentation, which is used by most educators to present educational content in terms of text or graphics. As a presentation tool, the Web has been used in a variety of ways. We can include live video, audio, multimedia, text, graphics, animation, interactivities, colors, and other presentation components to make the Web more presentable to accomplish educational tasks. Some additional components that make the Web an effective presentation tool include database for automated assessment and managing student information

The second feature of the Web that has the most promising capability is its communication and collaborative aspects. Originally, the Web was designed by Berners-Lee at CERN (The European Laboratory for Particle Physics in Geneva) to be a communication and collaborative tool to be used by six-thousand international scientists. There are several advanced technologies that are embedded in the design of the Web that allow for collaboration and communication. Some of these components include

- Chat area for social interaction and communication.
- Forum area for threaded discussion to provide assistance.
- FTP capability for transferring materials.
- Electronic mail for immediate feedback.
- Bulletin board for providing information and generating new ideas.
- Videoconferencing for live interaction.

As we shall see in later chapters, these tools make the Web an inquiry and project-based problem-solving tool that allows educators to develop educational settings that will promote meaningful learning.

The third feature of the Web is its information seeking capability. The Web as a research tool is often ignored in educational Web design. The search engines on the Web have provided remarkable tools for people seeking out new information. This aspect of the Web allows learners to become independent learners and to seek further information.

The fourth feature of the Web that can prove to be very constructive for educational purposes is its production capabilities. Students can learn to construct their own communities of learners. Such communities can include designing Web pages to present their products, designing content or project oriented Web sites, creating resources, and constructing communication and collaborative sites.

The central goal of this book is to discuss how the Web can be used as a reform tool to develop student-centered design that would satisfy the demands of the information overload, the challenges of diversity, and the contributions of learning theories. In order to achieve this goal, the full potential of the Web including its presentation, communication, research, and production features should be implemented to create curriculum that is student-centered.

Student-Centered Design

Therefore, let me argue that the actual dawn of user interface design first happened when computer designers finally noticed, not just that end users had functioning minds, but that a better understanding of how those minds worked would completely shift the paradigm of interaction. (Kay, 1989, p. 121)

In order to effectively use the Web as a reform tool to transform teaching and learning in the classroom to meet the new challenges of education, we need to adapt new instructional techniques that are student-centered. In this book student-centered design is defined as a process in which students' needs and backgrounds are placed at the heart of the design for e-learning environments. The first step towards developing effective e-learning environments is to have a clear understanding of how students' minds work when they perceive, store and retrieve instructional materials. Once we have a clear understanding of this process, then we can begin to use such knowledge to create technology based curriculum that is student-centered. Let's look at the phenomenon of understanding students' minds from a human information processing perspective where a student is engaged in a Web-based instructional unit.

Educational materials that are designed for e-learning environments can be viewed as the incoming multimedia information to be processed by the learner at two levels. First, there is the perceptual level, in which instructional materials are presented in terms of auditory, visual, interactivity, or the navigational modality. At this level the goal is to personalize the presentation of instructional materials (e.g. text, audio, video, screen design) to attract the learners' attention and make them focus on what they need to perceive. The second level of instructional processing is concerned with knowledge organization. This level is concerned with the way information is organized to be encoded with the student's prior knowledge and to be stored permanently in his/her memory in a meaningful manner. For example, information at this level can be organized according to teaching models that are the most appropriate to the educational goals of the given instructional unit or the types of learner. The goal at this level is to organize the instructional material according to the most appropriate teaching model and relate this new information to the learner's learning style or the type of academic content being presented.

There is nothing new about these two levels of processing information. Traditionally, the field of human computer interaction has based its methodology on human information processing as the theoretical model to support the perceptual and knowledge organization levels of information processing (Anderson, 1990, Preece, et al, 1995). We can use the same theoretical model for development of e-learning environments.

Figure 1.1 illustrates the main characteristics of a human information processing model. The boxes in Figure 1.1 represent how information, or instructional material, is processed and stored into long-term memory from one level to the next. First, information from the environment, in the form of instructional units, is filtered through the sensory register and is stored in short-term memory (Working Memory). Short-term memory is the active part of the students' memory. Whenever students are consciously thinking about something, they are using their short-term memory. Unfortunately, short-term memory is limited in two ways: capacity and duration. First, the students' short-term memory can hold only five to seven chunks of information (Miller, 1956). Second, short-term memory can only hold information for about 30 seconds. Therefore, information in short-term memory is selectively attended to base on the perception of the presented materials. If multimedia elements such as text, images, animation, color, or interactivity are selected and designed according to the students' personal preferences, then perception of these materials is made easy and students will focus their attention on instructional materials.

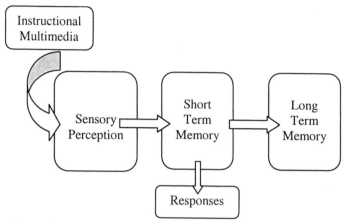

Figure 1.1 An Information-Processing Model of Learning

In order for information to be stored permanently in the mind of the learner, it has to be processed into long-term memory. Meaningful learning is said to take place when information is organized so that it can be properly encoded into long-term memory as knowledge or permanent memory. For this new knowledge to be useful and permanent, it must be encoded with the students' prior knowledge. The successful retrieval (output) of knowledge to solve problems depends on the way information is initially encoded into long-term memory. If encoding was performed properly, then, retrieval is automatic. On the contrary, if information was placed in the long-term memory without regard to prior knowledge or organization, then retrieval of information is very difficult if not impossible.

With the dramatic explosion of the Web for educational purposes, the interaction between learner and machine has entered a new phase of development where the design of perceptual and knowledge organization for instructional units plays a crucial role. The theoretical model of human information processing, if it is extended to satisfy the demands of student-centered design both at the perceptual level as well as the knowledge organization level, has wonderful implications for designers or teachers who wish to develop a student-centered curriculum for educational Web sites.

Dembo (1995) has suggested that human information processing theories can be extended to include an executive control unit within which perceptual and knowledge organization strategies can be embedded. These strategies for the perceptual level have a variety of functions such as focusing students' attention through presentation, and assisting students' storing information into long term-memory through appropriate organization of instructional materials. Figure 1.2 illustrates the expansion of basic human information processing by embedding perceptual and organizational strategies into its executive control unit. The flow of information from the environment into the perceptual design zone embodies a variety of cognitive strategies including perception, memory, interaction, visual design navigational systems, and attention. The perceptual design that is student-centered, therefore, accounts for the presentation of text, images, audio, color, or interactivity that are preferred by the learner's cognitive style. These aspects of design fall in the domain of interface design.

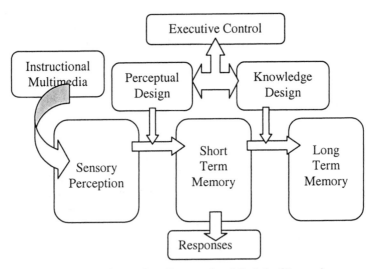

Figure 1.2 Information-Processing Model of Learning

The second process, as shown in Figure 1.2, is between working memory and the long-term memory, which attends to the organization of knowledge structures for instructional units. The flow of information into the knowledge design embodies a variety of different kinds of cognitive tasks that are concerned with identification, classification, organization, and elaboration of curriculum content. As mentioned before, such content must be properly encoded into the long-term memory so that retrieval for problem solving is facilitated. Proper encoding must be done according to the type of learning objectives as well as types of learner. Here the strategies for creating student–centered design pay attention to the application of learning theories and teaching models that are aligned with the learning style of the student.

In summary, in order for educational Web sites to be developed as student-centered, they must accurately account for the design of the perceptual level as well as the design of the knowledge organization level. These two levels expand the limitations of the information processing model and provide a research based theoretical framework that satisfies the needs of student-centered design for educational materials for the Web.

Structure of the Book

Building on the two features, perceptual level and knowledge organization level of the expanded version of the human information processing models, Figure 1.3 illustrates three areas of a student-centered design model for educational Web sites: perceptual design, knowledge design, and development and evaluation.

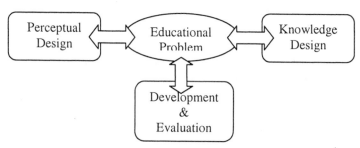

Figure 1.3 Areas of Instructional Technology Development

This book is designed to follow the knowledge one needs in each of the three areas, as illustrated in Figure 1.3, to develop an educational Web site. In addition to an introductory chapter, the book also has three parts:

Part I: Knowledge Design
Part II: Perceptual Design
Part III: Development and Evaluation

To give the readers a sense of the organization, the book starts with an introductory chapter (present chapter) with two purposes. First, it introduces the reader to new challenges facing education in the twenty-first century. Second, it sets the tone and the organization of the book. The remainder of the book is divided into three parts.

Part I deals with knowledge designs that are required for the way educational material is structured. The goal in this part is to identify learning theories that have direct implications for knowledge organization. The learning theories that are discussed in this part include

- Behavioral Theories and Structured Learning Environments
- Cognitive Theories and Constructive Learning Environments
- Social Theories and Social Learning Environments
- Psychological Theories and Thematic Learning Environments

Part II focuses on perceptual design and how to personalize the presentation of instructional materials to attract the learners' attention in order to make them focus on the instructional material. The goal of this part is to discuss the following design elements:

- The Foundations of Interface Design
- Visual Interface Design

- Psychology of Perception
- Visual Design Elements
- Design Techniques
- Educational Screen Design
- Information Architecture for Education

Part III deals with a model for development and evaluation of a project. The first step in development of an educational Web site is to identify the educational goal or the problem that needs solution and the target audience/students. Based on the educational goal and the needs of the target audience, decisions about perceptual and knowledge organization designs are made. The development process adheres to the following:

- Educational Goal.
- Planning of Student-Centered Design
- Development of Student-Centered Design
- Evaluation and Maintenance of Student-Centered Design

Reflection

Interactive e-learning environment design for education is an emerging instructional design field. It is stimulating and troublesome. It is stimulating because technology encourages teachers and designers to become architects of learning environments. It is troublesome because without adequate knowledge and a systematic approach, it may not fulfill its full potential. The challenge is to design e-learning environments from a multidisciplinary approach that provides effective learning environments for the students.

Ultimately, the goal of e-learning is to allow designers to develop environments that are educationally effective. Clearly not every person learns the same way and not every curriculum should be present in the same manner. Students are different in their learning styles, and different disciplines and contents require different presentation. For example, e-learning can provide an environment where music can be taught to a deaf person by the use of color patterns representing different notes. Then while the hearing students can hear Beethoven's Fifth from a CD, the deaf student can see patterns of the colors that represent the notes of Beethoven's Fifth on a CD-ROM. E-learning provides dynamic environments that can actually personalize instruction both in terms of learning styles and types of content being presented.

This book's approach is helpful in reaching the full potential of technology in education. It serves as a nexus to bring together the four distinct fields of emerging technology, learning theories, interface design, and instructional design as a unifying foundation for development of effective educational multimedia. To help you think ahead about the content of this book and to show you that different situations may require different types of learning, imagine that you are the educational technologist for a large school district. Four teachers have come to ask for your assistance to create e-learning environments for their classes. Each of the teachers has posed the following situation to ask you to work with them to design and develop e-learning environments for their classes. After reading each situation, think about how you would design the e-learning environments that would effectively solve the problems presented to you by the teachers in your district.

1. Mrs. Green is a high school chemistry teacher: She would like to use a Web site that teaches her students all the elements of the periodic table including memorizing symbols such as atomic numbers. Such a lesson would require a procedure for rote memorization and an assessment tool to ensure that students have mastered the educational goal of the Web site.

2. Mr. Ramirez is a middle school math teacher. He would like to allow his students to discover the Pythagorean theorem from a real world situation. How would you design a Web site that allows this? Such a Web site requires a guided discovery process that leads students to discover the Pythagorean theorem looking at real world problems.

3. Mrs. Gibson is a high school social science teacher. She would like to show her students that they could solve problems in a social context through discussion and make a collective and democratic decision. The situation is the race for the governor of the state where a company that has created a lot of jobs for the state is also polluting the environment. Students must look at the pros and cons of both sides, talk to experts, and discuss with each other in order to make a collective decision. Such a Web site would require a guided cooperative teaching model being implemented.

4. Mrs. Springfield teaches in a middle school where she works with other teachers to teach students through an interdisciplinary approach. She wishes to teach her students how science can help to save the rain forest in South America. She would like you to help her to develop a problem based interdisciplinary science unit with the theme of change. Such a Web site requires an understanding of how themes can be integrated into the design of curriculum to bring all the disciplines together. It further requires a clear understanding of what is involved in developing a problem based e-learning environment that is ideal for the Web.

The above problems are just representative of different teaching models suitable for different types of learning and different content areas. Please take note on how you would design and develop each. After reading each chapter in the book, you should come back to these questions and find the question that relates to the chapter you have read. Rethink how you would design e-learning curriculum for the appropriate question. Then compare your new notes with the old notes. You will notice some differences in the way you think about the design and development of e-learning environments.

Part I
Orientation to Learning Theories

Developing effective e-learning environment sites requires a clear understanding of how students learn. This will be accomplished by familiarizing ourselves with various learning theories that have posited how people learn. The learning theories that have been introduced by scholars like Skinner (1954), Piaget (1952), Vygotsky (1978, 1992), and Erikson (1950) can be instrumental in the development of e-learning environments that are based on how students learn. Over the years, the interest in learning theories and their application to educational technology has fluctuated. A brief explanation of the development of educational technology as it adapted itself to learning theories will provide the setting for the exploration of the themes that are discussed in the chapters of Part I

During the 1950's, partly because of the 1957 Sputnik launch by the Russians, the emphasis of educational programs focused on subject-oriented curriculum, which was based on behavioral learning theory. The leading behaviorist, B. F. Skinner (1954), advocated that learning was shaped by operant conditioning of the response through reinforcement. Instruction was considered to follow specific steps and procedures. Instructional units were broken into smaller and more manageable modules each with a specific object. Instructional modules were presented to the students. Successful evaluations of the modules lead the learner to the next step, and failure to achieve the objective resulted into going back to the instructional module.

This rigid and mechanical behavioral approach to education was ideal for the educational technologies of the 1960's and 1970's. The grand master of using technologies as a tool to reflect a behavioral approach is exemplified by the work of Patrick Suppes. Suppes and his colleagues began working at Stanford University in 1963 to develop technology based mathematical curriculum. Their work is closely linked to the educational technology that has become known as tutorial, or practice and drill. Chapter 2 is devoted to presenting how a systematic structuring of instruction was matched with a behavioral pedagogical approach to tutorials and drills that technology of the time could easily handle.

During the 1980's partly because of Piaget's research in cognition and developmental studies, the pendulum of education and educational technology swung toward developmentally appropriate programs and cognitive psychology. Piaget believed that children through interacting with the environment construct their own knowledge. This gave birth to a new movement in educational technology that collectively has come to be known as a constructivist approach.

Papert (1980) who was trained by Piaget took a constructivist approach to educational technology by developing computer based learning environments in which children could construct their own knowledge. Papert developed a computer language for children called LOGO that provided the learning environments for them to construct their own cognitive development. Papert also introduced another powerful idea for educational technology, Microworlds, in which children were actively involved in exploring certain abstract concepts. The first Microworld was Turtle Geometry, which was based on LOGO programming. The result of Papert's work is a strong recommendation to understand the cognitive development of the students first, and then apply their characteristics to develop interactive learning environments.

Fortunately, the influence of Papert in the area of educational technology coincided with the development of hypermedia and authoring tools, such as HyperCard, in the mid to late1980's. These new technologies revolutionized traditional modes of organizing information. Traditionally information structures, such as books and video, were organized as linear and sequential. Hypermedia allowed information to be organized as networks of nodes of information, where links allowed users to access non-sequential information with the click of a mouse. Such a dynamic organization of information was ideal for the constructivist approach to educational technology. Chapter 3 focuses on the discussion of a cognitive approach to the design of interactive e-learning environments.

Parallel to a cognitive constructivist approach, the contextual theory of learning, lead by Vygotsky's theory (1978, 1992) became an instrument of curriculum design and an educational technology approach. They argued that learning is contextual and a social event. The most appropriate approach to the design of educational technology, it was argued, is the development of problem-based education situated in the context of the real world. The Cognition and Technology Group at Vanderbilt University developed the Jasper Woodbury videos that provided a good example of problem solving in the real world.

Fortunately, with the advent of social constructivists, the technological revolution introduced the World Wide Web, which was ideal for development of socially based educational materials. The Web was first developed by Tim Breners at CERN (The European Laboratory for Particle Physics in Geneva) as a collaborative tool and a means of distributing information. It allowed structuring of information as hypertext that can be published on the Internet. By definition and function, the Web is a social tool and it is ideal for the application of a social constructivist approach. In Chapter 4, I shall discuss the application of a social cognitive theory to the design of Web-based instruction.

Another approach to educational technology is a thematic, interdisciplinary, and cooperative approach. This approach is very similar to social constructivism with a twist. This approach is guided by a theme that acts like glue that brings other disciplines together. For example, the *Great Ocean Rescue* CD-ROM, which was developed by Tom Snyder, applies a thematic, interdisciplinary approach to the development of an educational technology learning environment. As to be discussed in Chapter 5, a thematic approach can benefit from psychological theories that were posited by Eric Erikson.

These various points of view have been the subject of debates for many years. Adhering to a single principle of learning is not effective. A majority of psychologists, educators and instructional designers believe that a merger of various principles of learning should provide the bases of instructional design. By understanding different learning principles, effective educational Web sites or e-learning titles can be planned, designed, and developed that are conducive to the educational goals of the students.

The purpose of Part I is to describe several broad theories of learning that have been most influential in the field of instructional design. Four learning theories that include behavioral, cognitive/developmental, social, and psychological are presented in separate chapters, and their implications to educational technology are discussed in detail. Each chapter includes

- Detailed discussion of a theory of learning.
- Implication of the learning theory to teaching model(s).
- Implication of the theory to educational technology design.
- Discussion of one or two educational Web sites or multimedia units that are based on the learning theory.

Chapter 2
Behavioral Theories and E-Learning

The behavioral approach to learning and development, which has for the most part dominated the psychology of curriculum design and educational technology, has evolved from relying on a few basic principles. Despite various behavioral theories that extend from the simple classical conditioning of Ivan Pavlov to the elaborate operant conditioning of B. F. Skinner, all share common basic principles that have been used successfully in designing educational materials. The behaviorists believe that instruction should have a specific goal(s), and they strongly support sequencing of instructional materials by first presenting simple facts and then moving into more complex information. They believe that if teachers present and sequence instructional materials and evaluate students' achievements, then students will learn more effectively.

To have a clear understanding of the behavioral approach to education and the implications of its concepts to development of structured e-learning environments, I will discus the following topics in this chapter:

- Behavioral Theories
  - Pavlov's Classical Conditioning
  - Thorndike's Connectionism Theory
  - Skinner's Operant Conditioning
  - Applied Behavioral Analysis
  - Schedule of Reinforcement
- Application of Behaviorism to Models of Teaching
  - Mastery Learning Model
- Implication of Behaviorism to Development of E-Learning Environments
- Structured E-Learning Tutorials and NASA's *Virtual Skies*
  - Assessment (Determine the Main Goal)

- Breakdowns of the Main Goal into Subordinating Goals
- Determine the Events of Instruction for Each Subordinating Goal
- Intervention (Events of Instruction)
  - Presentation (Demonstrate New Concept)
  - Structured Practice (Practice, Provide Corrective Feedback)
  - Guided Practice (Independent Practice, Feedback)
- Evaluation

Pavlov's Classical Conditioning

Ivan Pavlov, a Russian scientist, in his work on the digestive system of dogs came upon an interesting idea that changed the history of psychological research. He was well aware of the fact that dogs salivate as a natural response to stimuli such as food. In his laboratory he created a situation where a bell was sounded a few seconds before a hungry dog was to be fed. After several attempts repeating the same process of sounding a bell before feeding, the dog began to salivate simply at the sound of the bell. Pavlov called the process by which the dog learned to respond to an artificial stimulus to provoke natural responses *classical conditioning.* The bell that originally had no meaning to the dog was referred to as the *conditioned stimulus* because of its association with food, and the salivation as the response to the sound of the bell as the *conditioned response.*

In his later works, Pavlov found that once a dog is conditioned to respond to the sound of a bell, it would also salivate to other sounds such as a siren or horn. He referred to this extended conditioned response as *stimulus generalization.*

Thorndike's Connectionism Theory

In the U.S., John B. Watson (1878-1958) and E.L. Thorndike (1874-1949) were influenced by Pavlov's classical conditioning and applied it to educational environments. Of these two American scholars, the work of E.L. Thorndike in the area of applying a behavioral approach to education dominated educational practices in the United States for several decades in the twentieth century.

Thorndike's theory of learning has come to be known as *Connectionism* because he posited that learning was a process of forming a connection between stimulus and response. Thorndike based his theory on an experiment he conducted on animals. He placed a cat in a cage where a string was hanging from the door into the cage. Food as a reward was placed outside the cage behind the door. The cat was placed in the cage and after extended trial and error found that pulling the string would open the door. By opening the door the cat had access to food or his reward. The process was repeated over and over again till the cat connected that pulling the string would open the door that resulted in a reward in terms of food. Based on this experiment on animals, Thorndike defined learning as habit formation, or forming a connection between stimulus and response.

Thorndike applied his connectionism theory directly into educational planning. He developed two major laws of learning that are influenced by reward: *law of effect* and *law of exercise.* Law of effect simply states that when a connection is created between stimulus and response and is followed by reward, the connection is strengthened (Thorndike, 1913).

> When a modifiable connection is made between a situation and a response and is accompanied or followed by a satisfying state of affairs, the strength of that connection is increased. When an annoying state of affairs goes with or follows a connection, the strength of that connection is decreased. (p. 71)

The second important principle posited by Thorndike for educational purposes was the law of exercise. This principle simply states that the strength of a stimulus-response connection is directly proportional to the number of times it has been repeated. In other words, the more practice the stronger the connection between the stimulus and response, and the less practice the weaker the connection between the stimulus and response.

Although Connectionism no longer enjoys the extreme popularity it once had in educational practices, one can easily observe the influence of Thorndike today in development of e-learning environments. The use of gold stars, points, and other extrinsic motivational tools as a reward system that was first introduced by Thorndike is now a milestone of educational CD-ROMs, Websites, and other e-learning environments. Also, the common process of practice and drill in educational software and multimedia titles, especially in tutorials, is a direct influence of the law of exercise.

Skinner's Operant Conditioning

Like other behaviorists, B. F. Skinner's learning and developmental theory, known as *operant conditioning*, was based on animal research. While other behaviorists experimented on dogs and cats, Skinner used rats and pigeons to carry out his experiments and then applied his animal behavior findings to human learning processes. As to be discussed in later chapters, the application of animal psychology to human learning may not always be a suitable ground for developing e-learning environments.

Skinner's behavioral theory (1953), however, differed in two major ways in relation to other behavioral theories. First, Skinner's theory differed in respect to stimuli-responses, and second his theory differed in the treatment of reward. In both treatments, Skinner's theory became more akin to explaining higher psychological functions that are uniquely human.

Skinner, like other behaviorists, believed that stimuli could cause responses in human behavior. However, he differs in his treatment of response in behavioral theory. Unlike Thorndike who believed that there is only one type of response, Skinner posited two different responses to explain human behavior. The two types of response are called *respondent* and *operant*. Respondents are responses that occur to a specific stimulus. This type of response is very similar to the way other behaviorist treated the definition of response. These types of response represent elementary needs. For example, you drink water (response) when you are thirsty (stimulus). However, a majority of human learning behavior, according to Skinner, is of the operant response type. Operant responses occur for no apparent reason, and they are uniquely human. For example reading a book, playing, or paying attention are operant responses that occur at random.

It is the operant responses that form the basis of Skinner's operant conditioning theory. According to Skinner there are certain responses that a human child has the innate propensity to acquire. These responses he referred to as operant responses. If the operant responses are properly reinforced, then they become rooted in human behavior. This is why Skinner refers to his theory as operant conditioning. Conditionings of the operant response become the goal of learning and education. For example, when a child in the first grade pays attention or reads a book, and the teacher smiles every time the student is paying attention or reading a book, then such behaviors are positively reinforced and become part of the behavioral repertoire of the child. Learning to pay attention or reading a book, as the result of smiles, is uniquely human behavior.

Skinner, very much like Thorndike, believed reward was the most important factor in the learning process. Skinner, however, preferred the term reinforcement in lieu of reward. To Skinner, reinforcement was a process that increased the probability of responses. Skinner (1986) states: " A reward is compensation or remuneration for services performed and is seldom immediately contingent on behavior. We reward people; we reinforce behavior" (p.106).

Table 2.1 shows there are two types of reinforcement and two types of punishment. Reinforcements increase the probability of a response occurring. The reinforcements can be either positive or negative. Positive reinforcement occurs when in following a particular response an action is performed to strengthen the response. For example, when a student performs his task in school, and the teacher reinforces the performance by saying "Good Job!", then the student is being positively reinforced. Negative reinforcement on the other hand occurs when in following an unpleasant response an action is taken to strengthen the response. For example, whenever there is a test for which a student always feigns illness and wishes to go to the nurse, and the teacher allows this, then the student is being negatively reinforced. This is because the student is getting his/her way by creating an unpleasant situation in the class, and the student's action is being reinforced by the teacher's response.

Table 2.1 Reinforcement and Punishment

Increase Responses	Decrease Responses
Positive: Strengthens pleasant responses and increases the probability of response.	Punishment 1: Weakens responses. It decreases bad behavior.
Negative: Strengthens unpleasant responses and increases the probability of response.	Punishment 2: Weakens responses. Reprimand.

There are also two types of punishment. Punishment decreases the probability of bad behavior. For example in punishment 1, a teacher says to a student who is constantly talking "You can not use the computer if you keep on talking." The teacher is punishing the student, thus decreasing the occurrence of bad behavior. In punishment 2, a student who is constantly talking in a classroom is told by the teacher "Will you please shut up?" The teacher is reprimanding the student. Punishing the student by reprimanding him/her weakens bad behavior.

Skinner is probably the most influential behaviorist. Numerous behavioral modification and instructional programs including mastery learning, educational software, programmed instruction, and computer-assisted instruction have been based on his operant conditioning and programmed instruction philosophy. In particular Skinner's contributions can be seen in the area of applied behavioral analysis and development of the schedule of reinforcement.

Applied Behavioral Analysis

The contributions of Skinner were influential on development of applied behavior analysis, which has been successfully used in treating educational problems and social problems such as anxiety and aggression. The basic principles of applied behavioral analysis can be used to solve educational problems. Skinner and other behaviorists strongly believed that students' educational problems must be assessed, and an instructional objective(s) should be written to treat the educational problem. After identifying the objective, the teacher should seek out the most logical sequence of instructional materials presented in small steps to treat the educational problem. If the students respond to the problem, then they must be immediately reinforced.

Figure 2.1 shows how applied behavior analysis can be modified in the area of learning.

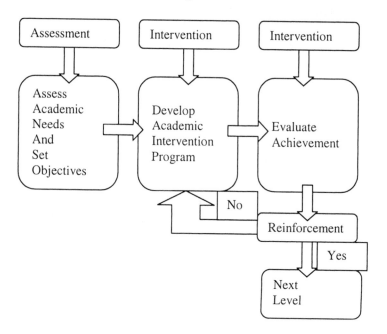

Figure 2.1 Educational Applied Behavior Analysis

As illustrated in the diagram in Figure 2.1, an effective applied behavior analysis for education has three components: assessment, intervention, and evaluation. The purpose of assessment is to pretest the learner's level and set the goal and objective. To achieve the objective(s), educators must develop an academic intervention program such as sequenced instructional materials and appropriate practice with feedback and reinforcements. Finally, the learners should be evaluated on their competencies in relation to the goal(s) that was set for the intervention. If responses on the evaluation are correct, then, the learner should be guided to the next level of instruction. If the learners cannot provide appropriate responses, then, they are guided back to the intervention component for further instruction.

Schedule of Reinforcement
The development of the schedule of reinforcement is the second area in which Skinner's theory of operant conditioning was influential. A schedule of reinforcement deals with when or how often a response is reinforced. From this perspective, reinforcement can either be continuous or intermittent. If reinforcement is continuous, it may not be as effective as intermittent, which can be applied either as a ratio or interval.

A ratio deals with reinforcing a portion of responses; for example, it can be a fixed reinforcement that is applied after each set of four appropriate responses. In this case the learner receives reinforcement after completing four problems. A ratio can also be set according to a variable. For example, it may be based on presenting the subject with reinforcement after an average number of responses such as 1:3 or 1:20. In this case it is very hard for the learner to predict when he or she gets reinforcement.

Intermittent reinforcement can also be an interval when reinforcing occurs following a lapse of time from the previous reinforcement. Interval reinforcement can also be fixed or variable. In a fixed interval there is a constant unit of time between the reinforcements; for example, students will be graded every five minutes when they are using the program. In variable intervals, reinforcement is presented after a lapse of time. The subject does not know when the next reinforcement is going to come.

Application of Behaviorism to Models of Teaching

The principles of behavioral theories and applied behavioral analysis have been successfully applied to the design of instruction. Numerous teaching models have been developed based on the principles of behavioral learning theories. Many of them such as Mastery Learning, Programmed Instruction, Personalized System of Instruction, Teaching to the Test, Direct Instruction Model, and the Condition of Learning have been successfully used in curriculum development. There are differences among these teaching models. However, most of them share some common characteristics that are derived from the principles of behavioral theories that include assessment, intervention, and evaluation.

One of the most suitable teaching models that has been developed based on behavioral theories and has direct application to educational technology is Mastery Learning. The success of this model is based on two principles. First, this model follows a structured and step-by-step approach to teaching. Second, it is assumed that any student can master educational concepts if adequate time is provided.

Mastery Learning Model

John B. Carroll (1963) formulated Mastery Learning or Direct Instruction, which has its origin in the behavioral family of teaching and Skinner's theory of operant conditioning. Mastery Learning assumes that all students can master the materials presented in the lesson. Carroll believed that all students have the aptitude to learn; however, he views aptitude as the amount of time that students devote to mastering the presented educational material. Mastery Learning follows the three components of applied behavioral analysis: assessment, intervention, and evaluation. First, the instructional design principles that were derived from Mastery Learning or Direct Instruction focus on assessing the instructional needs of the learner. Second, the intervention focuses on conceptualizing the learner's performance into goals and tasks. These tasks are then broken into smaller components for which instructional activities are developed. Each subcomponent must be mastered before the learner can go to the next task. These tasks are arranged in a sequence of learning that eventually leads the learner to master the original concept. Finally, the learner's achievement is evaluated.

Implication of Behaviorism to Development of E-Learning Environments

Patrick Suppes and his colleagues carried out an early application of behaviorism to technology at Stanford University. Suppes came out of a behavioral tradition during the early 1960's, and he is closely identified with a model of instruction called practice and drill. He believed in teaching school subjects (e.g. Mathematics) by breaking down the subject into strands that in turn, were divided into skill objectives. Each skill objective was presented and appropriate exercises were constructed. The computer managed the presentation of the skills, structured practice, and tracked correct and incorrect responses with appropriate feedback. Such an approach to using computers to present and provide corrective responses and feedback became known as practice and drill.

Suppes and his Stanford colleague (Atkinson) established the Computer Curriculum Corporation (CCC) in 1967. While Atkinson was responsible for developing reading materials for educational technology, Suppes concentrated on the design and development of mathematical units for use on computers. CCC became a very successful business endeavor.

There were several reasons for the success of the CCC as an educational technology enterprise. First, it focused on a behavioral research based teaching model that had proven to be effective. Second, the content area (e.g. mathematics) had been broken into smaller educational units that made curriculum much more manageable. Third, every lesson had an objective that was followed by presentation of teaching materials and an evaluation that had a measurable outcome. Evaluation of measurable outcome was very important during that time because teaching of the basics and accountability was at an all time high. Another interesting concept for the success of CCC was that teachers could use technology for one-to-one instruction without direct involvement. These aspects, in addition to innovation in the use of computers in teaching and learning, were instrumental in the success of CCC.

The initial approach by CCC to the design of computer-assisted instruction was very simple. Initially, all the materials produced were presented as text and followed by simple interaction. For example, a mathematical problem (such as 20 + 20 = _____) was presented to the student. Students were encouraged to type in the answer. If the answer given by the student was right, he/she was given a new exercise. If the answer given by the student was not right, some feedback (such as TRY AGAIN) was presented to the students. Generally if a student had failed to provide the answer by the third try, the computer would present the correct answer (e.g. 20 + 20 = 40) followed by TRY AGAIN and a restatement of the problem.

By 1977 the mathematical units produced by CCC consisted of 14 strands. Several revisions of these curriculums were released in 1984, 1994, and 1995. By the mid 1990's, the text version of the original materials included multimedia components with color graphics, use of the mouse, buttons, and other emerging technologies. By the mid 1990's, a majority of the mathematical units produced by CCC were based on the new standards of the National Council of Teachers of Mathematics (NCTM). Today, the new mathematical materials produced by CCC are called Math Concepts and Skills, and the new name for the company is Viacom. This is a highly successful company whose educational content according to the main page on their Web site includes "more than 1,600 learning objectives, together with a collection of diverse interactive exercises."
http://www.successmaker.com/Courses/c_awc_mcs.html

Mainly because of Suppes contributions, application of behaviorism to educational technology has become known as tutorials or practice and drill. These new and commercially available tutorials for educational technology programs are based on the principles of Mastery Learning. For example, *Math Blaster* and *Algebra Blaster* were developed using the basic principles of behavioral learning theories and a Mastery Learning model. These educational software became quite popular in schools because they were structured and were used as remedial programs.

Although most educational technology programs based on a behavioral approach separate tutorials from practice and drill, in this book I shall consider practice and drill as an essential part of tutorials. Therefore, tutorials are defined as instructional units that include all phases of a Mastery Learning model. Computer-assisted instruction, based on the behavioral concepts as practiced by Suppes in the 1960's, has come a long way. Today, most tutorials are sophisticated multimedia units either on a CD-ROM or Web site. However, the basic principles of a behavioral approach to learning still provide the foundations of these more modern e-learning tutorials. To illustrate the developmental process for e-learning tutorials, I will use an example of a more sophisticated Web site developed by NASA's Educational Technology Team.

Structured E-learning Tutorials and NASA's Virtual Skies

Development of e-learning tutorial programs, based on behavioral principles and a Mastery Learning model include the following steps:

- Assessment (Determine the main goal)
    - o Breakdowns of the main goal into subordinating goals
    - o Determine the events of instruction for each subordinating goal
- Intervention (Events of instruction)
    - o Presentation (Demonstrate new concept)
    - o Structured Practice (Practice, Provide corrective feedback)
    - o Guided Practice (Independent practice, Feedback)

- Evaluation

Assessment (Determine the Main Goal)

According to Knirk and Gustafson (1986), the first step to determine the instructional goal is the process of assessing the current educational state and defining the desired goal. The gap between the two states, what is and what is desired, defines the instructional goal for e-learning environments. For example, if the average math level of a seventh grader is pre-algebra and the goal is to teach algebraic equations, then the discrepancy between the two levels provides the educational problem that needs to be solved by the development of an e-learning environment. Once the educational goal of an e-learning environment has been determined, then the producer has an excellent idea in how to plan for a site that will serve the needs of the students to achieve the stated goal(s).

Breakdowns of the Main Goal into Subordinating Goals

Once the main educational goal has been decided, the next step is dividing it into an appropriate number of subordinating goals. It is essential to flowchart the division of the main goal into subordinating goals. Figure 2.2 illustrate a flow chart for breaking down the main goal.

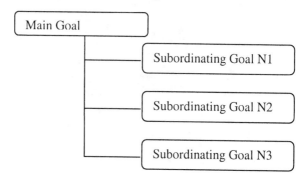

Figure 2.2 Flowchart of the Main Goal into Subordinating Goals

To illustrate the division of the main goal into subordinating goals, let's review an example. Figure 2.3 shows a snapshot of a Web site, developed by NASA, called *Virtual Skies*.
http://virtualskies.arc.nasa.gov/vsmenu/vsmenu.html
The goals of this rather comprehensive Web site on aviation and the US air traffic management system are as follow:

- To increase the user/learner's awareness of aviation research and contributions made by the National Aeronautics and Space Administration (NASA) and the Federal Aviation Administration (FAA).
- To explore the world of aviation and air traffic management.

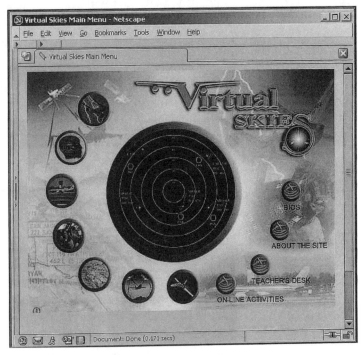

Figure 2. 3 Virtual Skies

Using a behavioral approach at various levels within its format, the *Virtual Skies* Web site blends text, animation and interactive graphics with a mix of lower cognitive level and critical thinking activities that mirror real world experience in the career fields related to aviation and air traffic management. At first glance the subordinating goals are not immediately identifiable. However, mousing over each circular image on the orientation (or opening) page reveals the following subordinating goals: Aviation, Weather, Aviation Research, Airport Design, Air Traffic Management, Navigation, Communication, and Aeronautics.

Intervention (Events of Instruction)
The purpose of phases in teaching models, such as Mastery Learning, is to establish the events of instruction for each subordinating goal. As mentioned before, the phases of instruction for Mastery Learning include Presentation, Structured Practice (Practice, Provide corrective feedback), and Guided Practice (Independent practice, Feedback). Figure 2.4 illustrates a generic flowchart for breaking down the main goal into subordinating goals with appropriate events of instruction.

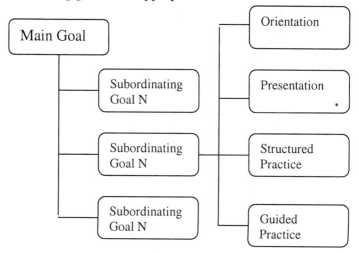

Figure 2.4 Flowchart of Main Goal/Subordinating Goals and Events of Instruction

Continuing on with NASA's *Virtual Skies*, by clicking on one of the 7 circular images, the learner enters a subordinating goal or content section. Within each content section, the learner is allowed to explore the content in greater depth as he/she strives to accomplish the learning goals. The opening page to each content section introduces the learner to the skills, concepts and processes to be covered as well as to the learning goals. Each of the subordinating goals (or content sections) breaks down into a series of four instructional events: Tutorials, Take Control, You Decide, and Certification. These four events of instruction in *Virtual Skies* closely parallel the four events of instruction in the Mastery Learning model. Table 2.2 shows the similarities of the events of instruction in *Virtual Skies* and events of instruction from the Mastery Learning model.

Table 2.2 Comparison

Virtual Skies	Mastery Learning Model
Tutorial: Concepts are presented with a static or interactive graphic or an animation with sound.	Presentation
Take Control: Learners are given choices to engage in critical thinking activities similar to the type of tasks workers in an aviation-related career field undertake.	Structured Practice
You Decide: Learners are encouraged to solve a real world problem related to the content found in the Tutorial.	Guided Practice

In order to provide some guidelines for teachers and instructional designers on how to apply a behavioral approach to structured e-learning, I will discuss in some detail how the four phases of the events of instruction from a Mastery Learning

Model have been applied to the *Virtual Skies* Web site. I should note here that in the applied behavioral model that was presented earlier, evaluation was a separate component of the model. The *Virtual Skies* Web site considers evaluation (certification) as part of intervention. To be consistent with the model, I shall first discuss the events of instruction, which are part of the intervention component in the applied behavioral model. Then, I will discuss evaluation as a separate component. In either case the process is the same.

Presentation (Demonstrate New Concept)

The first step in the events of instruction is conceptual presentation. New concepts may be presented by text, graphics, or animation. For example, on the NASA *Virtual Skies* Web site, the presentation of skills, concepts, and processes to be acquired are text-based and enhanced with explanatory animation with sound as well as interactive graphics. For example, in the content section Navigation, by viewing animation with sound, the user/learner sees how the Pythagorean theorem applies to an airplane's navigation from its departure point to its destination point while accounting for the effects of wind on its flight path.

Accessing the Weather content section of the same NASA Web site, the user/learner is treated to many meteorological concepts illustrated with static or interactive graphics. The latter encourages the user/learner to actively engage in visualizing the concepts being presented by clicking on a button or an object within a picture to activate such things as a change in temperature, a change in wind direction or a change in weather. Figure 2.5 illustrates graphics as the main context for presenting information about weather.
http://virtualskies.arc.nasa.gov/main/mweather.html
As the user clicks on the word "Day," graphics change and new graphics about weather and "Sea Breeze" are presented.

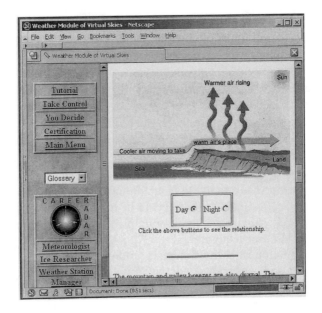

Figure 2.5 Illustrates Change of Graphics about Sea Breeze

Animation is also an effective type of conceptual presentation. For example, go to another Web site developed by NASA called *A Fierce Force of Nature: Hurricane.*

http://observe.arc.nasa.gov/nasa/earth/hurricane/intro.html

This site shows through animation how hurricanes start out as a group of storms that begin to rotate when they encounter converging winds.

Structured Practice and Guided Practice
Ideally, practice should be embedded in the tutorial following the initial conceptual presentation and guide the learner through acquisition of knowledge. This would follow the Mastery Learning teaching model that behavioral theorists have proposed for instruction. The cycle in which practice is presented is simple and initially follows two options:

- The learner follows through guided practice with help.
- The learner follows independent practice.

Most tutorial programs such as *Math Blaster* or *Algebra Blaster* provide both the guided and independent practice and drill. For example, Figure 2.6 shows how Math Blaster provides an initial option to the learner. Once the choice has been made, these programs present problems in subject matter (e.g. mathematics) and solicit responses.

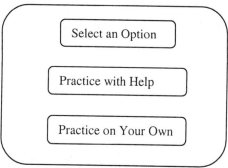

Figure 2.6 Providing Options to the Learner

To continue with the NASA Web site example *Virtual Skies*, both structured and guided practices are provided in a variety of ways and at varying cognitive levels. The Take Control phase provides structured practice and varies from a basic recall format to a synthesis level activity. Using basic recall practice in the Communication segment, for example, learners can practice learning the phonetic alphabet. Given a letter of the alphabet, a learner types in the phonetic alphabet word designating that letter (that is, "B" would illicit the correct response of "Bravo") Through a basic recall function, such knowledge will facilitate more accurate communication between pilots and controllers. Another Take Control activity, this one located in the Weather content section, offers practice in cloud type identification. A photo of a cloud is given. The user/learner is provided four possible responses of which only one is correct. A Hint button is also provided which gives the user/learner a text-based description that hopefully serves to trigger a memory synapse that identifies the cloud type correctly. Operating at a higher cognitive level (synthesis and evaluation), the learner is given a static radar screen with up to 6 aircraft targets and their data tags. Learners are asked to activate a button that provides an audio of a pilot request for a change in course (any single or combination) of altitude, speed and direction. The user/learner must read each aircraft's data tag to ascertain whether such a course change should be confirmed or denied based upon safe spacing rules, predicted flight paths, altitudes, and air speeds of all other aircraft targets on the radar screen.

Using another *Virtual Skies* example, the You Decide segment of the Airport Design content section serves as a guided practice piece. Here the user/learner employs the vast amount of knowledge gained from the Tutorial to sift through data and information to make a decision about where a new airport should be placed within a region portrayed on a fictional map. This independent practice calls into play many levels of cognition from comprehension through synthesis to evaluation, yet all the while providing the user/learner with an adequate amount of practice to master the skills, concepts and processes identified in the goals.

Fortunately, in recent years the structured and guided practice of the Mastery Learning teaching model has been presented in other ways. To continue with the *Virtual Skies* example, the team that has developed this Web site provides practice as exercises that they call Take Control and You Decide. The practice section called Take Control is similar to guided practice because it provides some hints. For example, Figure 2.7 illustrates that there is a button in the Take Control practice, called Hints if the learner needs some guidance. Similarly, in the same example, the button You Decide represents independent practice.

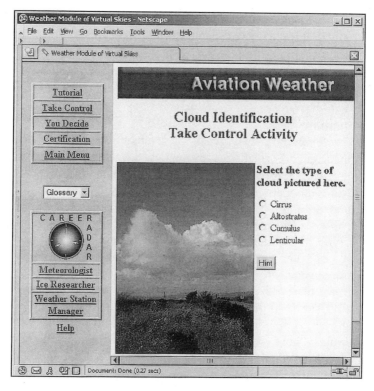

Figure 2.7 Take Control Exercise as Guided Practice

One of the most significant aspects of structured as well as guided practice is the reinforcement that is given after the learner provides a response. Reinforcement can be verbal, non-verbal (e.g. gold star, bonus points), or other extrinsic motivating resources. Effective tutorials follow a schedule of reinforcement as was previously discussed. For example, it may be based on presenting the subject with reinforcement after an average number of responses such as 1:3 or 1:20. In this case it is very hard for the learner to predict when he or she gets reinforcement. There are some general rules one can apply for reinforcement as follow:

- In teaching new tasks, reinforce immediately.

- In teaching new tasks reinforce continuously.
- Reinforce improvement. Do not expect perfection.
- Do not reinforce undesirable responses.
- More specific reinforcements should follow the intermittent.
-

Evaluation

There are two types of evaluations: formative and summative. Formative evaluation measures students' achievement before or during instruction. Summative evaluation measures students' achievement at the end of instruction. Most tutorial programs have formative evaluation as part of guided and independent practice. As discussed in the previous section, this type of evaluation is an ongoing process where students' responses are continuously judged, and feedback and reinforcement are provided according to a schedule of reinforcement with different types of reinforcement.

The final phase of the flow of instruction, based on the Mastery Learning model, is the summative evaluation, which determines how well students have attained the instructional objectives of the subordinating goals. Most tutorial programs have specific objectives that are set at the beginning of the program. These objectives usually have a specific percentage of a summative evaluation that the students must achieve. For example, the objective may have stated "After having completed the unit on one-step equations, the student will be able to answer correctly 90% of the questions on the assessment." Based on the percentage set in the objective, the student's achievement is evaluated. If the student achieves below 90%, the program will guide the student to the first presentation phase of the teaching model. On the other hand if the student scores above 90%, the program assumes that he/she has mastered the objectives of the subordinating goal; therefore, it will guide the student to the next level or the next subordinating goal of the program. This process is continued till all the objectives of the main goal have been achieved.

The clever team who designed *Virtual Skies* refers to the summative evaluation as "Certification." I shall reprint their certification here.

Certification

> After you have completed the Communication "Tutorial," have engaged in the activities found in the "Take Control" sub-section, and have spent time on the activities assigned to you by your teacher, you should be well prepared for the "Certification" process. This process consists of a multiple-choice quiz that you answer on-line. You must pass this quiz with 80% or better correct. If you do not receive at least 80% correct, you will be prompted on what to do next. But, you know that you should then review the "Tutorial" section again, don't you? If you do receive at least 80% correct, you will receive a certificate signifying that you have successfully progressed through the "Communication" section of VIRTUAL SKIES and are on your way toward participating in the VIRTUAL SKIES Collaborative Project. After successfully passing the quiz and receiving your Communication Certificate, you may continue to the next module. Good luck!

Reflection

Before closing this chapter, it is essential to write a few words about the behavioral approach to the design of multimedia learning environments. Tutorials and practice and drill, as adapted to educational technology, have received a lot of criticism. There is a growing number of educational technology theorists who claim that practice and drill is not the best use of technology. For example, Jonassen (1988) has criticized practice and drill programs for not using the full potential of computers. He claims that most practice and drill programs that are developed for computers can easily be done with pencil and paper, but there are those who support a practice and drill approach to technology (Salisbury, 1990) because they believe it is more efficient and a less costly way of teaching and learning.

What is important to remember is that numerous successful instructional materials have been developed using a behavioral approach. These successful programs usually are limited to text based instructional programs. The success of the text based instructional materials is primarily due to innovation and the effective instructional principles utilized. The same approach can be applied to e-learning environments. As we have seen in this chapter, *Virtual Skies* is a clear example of successfully applying a behavioral approach and Mastery Learning model to the design of a Web site.

There is definitely a place for the use of a behavioral approach to e-learning. There are situations in which application of the principles of behavioral theories is the best approach to the development of e-learning environments. The most important thing to remember about the design of e-learning environments is to gather adequate information about the target audience and the content, and then make an intelligent decision about what teaching model should be implemented in the actual development of the project. If a behavioral approach is the most suited for the project, then it must be implemented. For example, based on the content of this chapter, think about how you would design a Web site or a CD-ROM about the following content areas:

- Step by step lesson on "Balancing Chemical Equations".
- A lesson on teaching "Two Equations, Two Unknowns".
- Lesson on memorizing "Capitals of States".
- Multiplication Table.
- A lesson on teaching "Structure of a Biological Cell".
- A unit on teaching new Spanish Vocabulary.
- A unit on teaching the writing of simple numbers 1-9.
- A unit on components of the human brain.

Chapter 3
Cognitive Theories and E-learning

Just as children undergo remarkable physical changes during their development, their cognitive abilities also progress through fundamental transformations. Cognitive development refers to a mental process by which knowledge is acquired, stored, and retrieved to solve problems. Therefore, cognitive developmental theories attempt to explain cognitive activities that contribute to children's intellectual development and their capacity to learn. Cognitive developmental research has had a great impact on the constructivism movement in education and educational technology. In order to appreciate how cognitive developmental theories have contributed to the design, process, and development of constructive e-learning environments, I shall discuss the following topics in the remainder of this chapter:

- Piaget's Cognitive Developmental Theory
  o Schema, Assimilation, Accommodation, and Equilibrium
- Neo-Piagetian Theories
- Application of Cognitive Theories to Models of Teaching
  o Inquiry-Training
  o Discovery Learning
- Implication of Cognitive Theories to E-Learning
  o Inquiry-Training and Hypermedia
    ▪ NASA's Astro-Venture
  o Discovery Learning and Simulation
    ▪ NASA's Solar System Simulator

Piaget's Cognitive Developmental Theory
Piaget (1952) argued that children must continually reconstruct their own knowledge through active reflection on objects and events till they eventually achieve an adult perspective. Piaget (1952) posited that the process of intellectual

and cognitive development is mental adaptation to environmental demands. To have a better appreciation of this process, it is essential to understand four other concepts that Piaget has proposed. These concepts are *schema, assimilation, accommodation*, and *equilibrium*.

Schema

Piaget (1952) used the word schema to represent a mental structure that adapts to environmental patterns. In other words, schemata are intellectual structures, in terms of neuron assemblies or cell assemblies, that organize perceived events and group them according to common patterns. Schemata can be thought of as a series of interrelated index cards that represent different environmental patterns in one's mental structure. For example, a child might confuse a cow with a dog by calling it a doggie because the child at this stage of development has internalized in terms of cell assemblies a collection of features as a pattern that constitutes the schema of animals. Such patterns may include features like four legs, long ears, and non-human sounds. Table 3.1 shows a systematic way of organizing these features. If a feature has a plus it signifies its presence, and if the feature is negative the feature is absent in the pattern.

Table 3.1

	Four legs	Long ears	Tail
Dog	+	+	+
Cow	+	+	+

A child who has internalized these features would call a cow and a dog by the same name doggie, because both animals share the same pattern that includes all these features. However, as more features are detected from the environment, the child may differentiate between the sound of a dog and the sound of a cow or by their relative sizes. Furthermore, the child may differentiate between the presence or absence of horns between the two animals. The addition to and combination of these features to form new patterns in terms of cell assemblies would allow the child to differentiate between a dog and a cow. It should be mentioned that the new patterns for recognition of a cow and a dog are still under the dominance of a more general pattern for animals. Therefore, as children develop, their schemata become broader, more differentiated, and interrelated (Piaget, 1952).

There is ample evidence in research from neuroscience that shows there are two different ways that synaptic connections in neuron assemblies are formed after birth as the result of an individual's interaction with the environment. These synaptic connections are called *refinement and addition.* In the refinement process the brain mechanism first overproduces the number of synaptic connections to respond to general experience and environmental input (Bransford, J., et al., 1999 p. 104). As the result of more environmental input, these overproduced connections are selectively eliminated or reorganized due to personal experiences as children mature and develop their own cognitive abilities. The second way that brain plasticity allows the formation of synaptic connections in response to experiences is through the addition of new connections (Bransford, J., et al., 1999, p. 105). As the child matures, his personal experience in reaction to the social environment drives the brain mechanism to create more synaptic connections.

The process of the refinement of synaptic connections correlates to Piaget's concept of schema. Children come into any new learning environment with their own schemata that are representative of their patterns of life experiences and prior knowledge. A number of researchers (Anderson & Pearson, 1984; Piaget, 1952) have posited that schemata are the building blocks of intellectual development. During cognitive development, children's schemata are constantly restructured as they encounter new patterns in their learning experiences. Pearson and Sapiro in the May 1982 issue of *Instructor*, have provided one of the earliest and probably the best explanations of schema theory for instructional purposes:

> What is a schema?   It's the little picture or
> associations you conjure up in your mind when you

hear or read a word or a sentence. You can have a schema for objects (chair, boat, and fan), an abstract idea of feeling (love, hate, hope), an action (dancing and buying), or an event (election, garage sale, and concert). It's like a concept but broader. For example, you see the word tree and you conjure up the concept of a tree-trunk, branches, leaves, and so on. Your schema for a tree includes all this, plus anything else you associate with trees -- walks down country lanes, Christmas trees, birds' nests, and so on. A schema includes behavioral sequences, too. For example, your schema for the word party could include not only food, friends, and music, but also what you will wear, how you will get there, how long you plan to stay, and so on. And, of course, your schema for party is based on your experience at party, which may differ substantially from some one else's. Schema is an abstraction of experience that you are constantly fine-tuning and restructuring according to new information you receive. In other words, the more parties you attend the more schema adjustment you'll make. (p. 46)

Schema is not limited to concepts or objects and their relationships. There are also procedural schemata (Anderson & Pearson, 1984) that are the ways of processing information. For example, a child who has acquired the pattern of four sides for geometric shapes like a square or rectangle has internalized the data schemata about these shapes. However, as they grow they gain new mathematical patterns about areas and perimeter; these are procedural schemata. Both data and procedural schemata are constantly restructured in new learning environments. It is interesting to note that the concepts of data and procedural schemata correlate with types of taxon and locale memory (see Chapter 1) that were proposed by O'Keefe and Nadal (1978).

Assimilation, Accommodation, and Equilibrium

One of the most fundamental questions about schemata are how do changes in relationship to newly discovered patterns in the environment actually occur in the cognitive structure of children. Piaget was a biologist by academic training. He was very comfortable with the concept of adaptation to environmental stimuli. For example, the human body is structured to be constantly in a state of *equilibrium* in regard to its temperature. When the body temperature is raised by a few degrees during exercise, the entire system goes into a state of disequilibrium. The feedback mechanism senses such a state of disequilibrium and responds by producing sweat and sending more blood near the skin to cool the body down, thus restoring a state of equilibrium for the body.

Piaget used the same concept of biological *equilibrium-disequilibrium* states to explain the causes of cognitive reorganization in response to new learning experiences. When the child encounters a new learning environment or a new situation with which the pattern he or she is not familiar, a state of disequilibrium is created within the child's brain that must be internally managed. In order to create a comfortable state of equilibrium in the mental schemata, the child has to modify or restructure his or her schemata to account for the new situation. The internal mental mechanism or processes that are responsible for the restructuring of the child's schemata are *assimilation* and *accommodation* (Piaget, 1952, 1964).

Integrating new information with existing knowledge is a cognitive process that Piaget calls assimilation. As children are faced with new learning situations, they use their prior knowledge to make the new experience understandable. Prior knowledge is subsequently restructured to make a new experience fit in the newly formed schema. The change that occurs in the mental structure of the child is referred to as accommodation by Piaget (1952).

Piaget argued that, as learners assimilate input from the environment, the new information is not simply stored in the mind like information in files in a filing cabinet. Rather new information is integrated and interrelated with the knowledge structure that already exists in the mind of the child. "Every schema is coordinated with other schemata and itself constitutes a totality with differentiation parts" (Piaget, 1952. P. 7).

For example, in teaching geometry, when a pentagon is introduced to children, the salient features of this geometric shape such as sides and angles are not simply memorized. Rather, it is contrasted and integrated with what is already known about other geometric shapes like rectangles, triangles and squares. In other words, the schemata for a pentagon includes, in addition to its shape, sides, and angles, such related concepts as how its shape compares with other geometric shapes, how its angles compare with other geometric shapes, or how its area and perimeter differ from other geometric shapes. Learning in this manner of relating prior knowledge to new information is said to be meaningful because new schemata in the child's mental capacity have been formed. It is interesting to note how Piaget's explanation of schema, assimilation and accommodation correlates with synaptic connections that Bransford (1999) calls refinement and addition.

The process of cognitive development is the result of a series of related assimilations and accommodations. Conceptually, cognitive development and growth proceeds in this fashion at all levels of development from birth to adulthood (Piaget, 1964). However, because of biological maturation, major and distinctive cognitive development occurs over a lifetime. Piaget (1964) posited four major stages of cognitive development that occur over a lifetime. These stages are sequential, and successive stages are attained through changes in one's ability to internalize or mentally to organize prior knowledge with new information. Note that the process is still that of reorganizing cognitive abilities. According to Piaget, these stages are

Sensorimotor:	Birth to 2 years old
Pre-operational:	2 to 7 years old
Concrete operation:	7 years to adolescence
Formal operation:	Adolescence to adult

Sensorimotor refers to the stage that begins with the reflex actions of infants and proceeds through the development of basic concepts such as time, space, and causality. The end of the sensorimotor stage is characterized by the development of eye-hand coordination and spatial relationships, an understanding that objects still exist even when out of sight (object permanence), and the beginning of symbolic thought. At this point of development, children see themselves at the center of all actions in the world (egocentric). The effective coordination of these activity-dependent skills culminates in a concrete understanding of cause and effect and the internalization of sequences of actions that stand for or symbolize objects (e.g., seeing the table being set means dinner is on the way). This behavior marks the transition to the next stage of development.

The pre-operational stage is characterized by the development of symbolic thinking. Objects and events in the child's environment become represented by symbols. Language development is one of the major cognitive developments during this stage.

The concrete operational stage is marked by a significant increase in a child's ability to analyze and to classify patterns according to the attributes of objects or events. Piaget's extensive research shows that children in this stage learn to reverse procedure and to generalize the outcome of certain experiments. Reversal and generalization are the two essential cognitive abilities that enable children to learn the classification of objects, events and other concepts. The difficulty that children have at this stage relates to their inability to deal with abstraction. Children, however, gradually learn to deal with abstraction, and this leads their development to the next stage.

The formal operational stage of development generally begins in early adolescence and continues through adulthood. Formal reasoning is characterized by the ability to carry out mental activity using imagined and conditional actions and symbols that are divorced from their physical representation. Individuals at this stage are able to control variables systematically, test hypotheses, and generalize results to future occurrences. This stage, which continues to develop well into adulthood, is characterized by the ability to reason and solve problems. I shall discuss this stage more in detail later when the implications of cognitive developmental theories to models of teaching in reference to the inquiry-training model are presented.

Neo-Piagetian Theories

Many researchers in the field of cognitive development agree with the basic principles that Piaget has posited about cognitive development. However, Piaget's adherence to a stage-like theory of development came under heavy criticism. For example Bruner is well known for saying, "Any subject can be taught effectively in some intellectually honest form to any child at any stage of development" (Bruner, 1960, p. 52). Such a radical statement is in reference to Piaget's stage development theory that states development precedes learning. One must remember that Piaget did not in fact strictly adhere to his own theory of stages; after all, he published his first abstract and scholarly article at age eleven when he was still in his concrete operation stage. Such a practice of course denies the strict adherence to distinct stages for learning.

Piaget has also been criticized for underestimating the ability of children to think abstractly (Flavell, 1985). There is evidence that children before the formal stage, are capable of symbolic thinking, which is indicative of intellectual ability far earlier than the stage Piaget has posited. There are other cognitive psychologists who have contributed to the understanding of cognitive learning theories by modifying and expanding Piaget's' original theory to address these criticisms. The most dominant among these researchers are Ausubel (1963), Bruner (1966), and (Flavell, 1985).

Ausubel (1968) expressed the view that each discipline has a structure that is organized hierarchically. He described the mind as an information processing and information storing system that can be compared to the conceptual structure of an academic discipline. That is, there is a general structure in each discipline that is subconsciously known by the expert. These structures act like a map or web of knowledge where the more concrete aspects, such as facts and figures, of a discipline can be attached to the nodes of the hierarchical structure. Ausubel's approach certainly provides a way of explaining Piaget's concept of encoding prior knowledge with the new knowledge.

Ausubel came up with a new teaching approach that he called *Advance Organizer*. In this approach, he maintained that new ideas could be usefully learned and retained only if students are presented with an advance organizer that would map the structure of the discipline.

Jerome Bruner (1966) proposed a learning theory whose educational implications resemble the concrete to abstract concept of Piaget. Such a process is called *scaffolding* where initially the adolescent is dealing with concrete subjects, and the mentor provides a great amount of support. However, as the child learns more about the concept and begins to think abstractly, the support fades away. Bruner (1966) proposed that new concepts in education should be introduced to the students using three levels of presentation:

- *Enactive*: Use of concrete models of concepts and procedures.
- *Iconic*: Use of graphic representations of concepts and procedures.
- *Symbolic*: Use of abstract symbols and models to represent concepts and procedures.

In Bruner's theory, the support at the enactive level is concrete, at the iconic level it is visual, and at the symbolic level it is abstract. Such a theory of learning encourages increasing mental activities, abstract thinking, and problem solving at the higher levels.

In addition to his theory of instruction, Bruner (1960), like Ausubel, also argued for a new concept that each discipline has its own structure that can be taught to students. "Grasping the structure of a subject is understanding it in a way that permits many other things to be related to it meaningfully. To learn structure, in short, is to learn how things are related...." (Bruner, 1960, P.7). These structures are web like, and they are specific to different disciplines. Learning a new concept is meaningful only if it is attached to the appropriate nodes of these structures.

Another influential scholar who has continued Piaget's work in the area of cognitive development is Flavell. Flavell (1983) has provided a detailed discussion of three operations that adolescents gradually acquire during the formal operation of their development: *combinational reasoning, propositional reasoning and hypothetical-deductive reasoning*

Combinational reasoning refers to the ability of the adolescent to consider several different factors at the same time to solve a problem. This reasoning power provides the child with the ability to look at problems from an integrated approach. During the earlier stage, children are not capable of integrating several theories to solve problems: They can only deal with problems from one angle at a time.

Propositional reasoning refers to the characteristic that young adolescents acquire to reason on the basis of assumption and proposition to solve problems. For example, if a child during the concrete operational stage were asked to assume that coal is white, he would respond that coal is black and cannot be white. However, the young adolescent during the formal operation stage acquires the capability of proposition to solve problems that he would not have been able to solve during the concrete stage. This ability also extends to abstract thinking that is acquired during the formal stage.

Hypothetical-deductive reasoning allows the young adolescent to consider different hypotheses in dealing with a problem. Consideration of different hypotheses also enables the young adolescent to gather data and test different hypotheses to come up with a possible solution.

To use a simple example of how adolescents follow hypothetical-deductive reasoning in everyday life, let's consider a young 15-year-old girl who is going on her first date. In order to get ready for her date, the young lady goes into her room and gathers several different colored blouses and matching pants. She puts on a blouse and tries it with different colored pants while looking at her choice in the mirror, and then she tries another blouse with different pants. After several tries, she decides to wear the pretty blue blouse with the black pants. This process of selection of what to wear is natural to most young people. The instructional implication of such a procedure is significant. What the young lady has learned to do because of her recent development of hypothetical-deductive reasoning is that she has a problem to solve. In order to solve this problem, she first hypothesizes something about her taste in what looks good. Then she gathers information (her clothes). She then tests her hypotheses that some colors may go with others. She tests every one of her choices in color. She either accepts or rejects her choices. She makes a final decision as to what looks good for her date. The final selection is the result of careful analysis, testing, and accepting the result.

The above scenario may be a simplistic explanation of hypothetical-deductive reasoning. However, it is exactly what adolescents and scientists do in the process of solving problems. The process of hypothetical-deductive reasoning has provided the foundations of the *inquiry-training* model.

Application of Cognitive Theories to Models of Teaching

Piaget posited a useful theory to explain how, why, and when children develop and learn new concepts. His theory provides a frame of reference by which educators and educational technologists can analyze the behavior of the learner and design educational environments within which children can construct their own knowledge. Piaget never specified a set of steps or procedures for teaching. He provided a set of universal guidelines, his theory of learning, upon which one can design and plan for educational activities. It was left to the educators and educational planners to interpret his universal guidelines about cognitive development. In other words, he provided the learning environment with his theory for teachers to explore and then construct their own teaching methodology, strategies, and models. This is the central tenet of Piaget's thinking that individuals construct their knowledge of the world. And this is exactly the major driving force behind the constructivism movement in the US.

Cognitive and developmental psychologists, Piaget in particular, viewed learning as a dynamic process where learners construct their own knowledge by interacting with the world. The role of teachers, they believe, is not to impose steps, procedures, and rigid structure, but rather to be the architect for learning environments that facilitate a process in which students would be able to construct their own knowledge. This radical approach gave rise to a new group of educators and technologists who became collectively known as constructivists. Piaget's influence upon the constructivist's movement in the U.S. had a great impact on instructional design, teaching models, and educational technology. The main impact of constructivism can be seen mostly in inquiry-training and *discovery learning.*

Inquiry-Training

Suchmann (1962) who was quite familiar with Piaget's theory of cognitive development proposed an inquiry-training model for instruction in school. The general goal of inquiry-training is to help students develop a sense of the independent inquiry method, but in a disciplined way. It is interesting to note that the process of the inquiry-training model is similar to the description that Flavell (1983) proposed to explain the three operations of the formal operation. As mentioned before, hypothetical-deductive reasoning allows the young adolescent to consider different hypotheses in dealing with a problem. Consideration of different hypotheses also enables the young adolescent to gather data and test different hypotheses to come up with a possible solution.

The inquiry-training model of teaching has the following five phases of instruction:

1. Phase One: Puzzlement or intellectual confrontation by presenting students with a problem to create a state of disequilibrium in their mind.
2. Phase Two: Students will hypothesize a reason for the puzzlement.
3. Phase Three: Students will gather new information in regard to the hypothesis. Then they isolate relevant

information, eliminate irrelevant information, and organize them.

4. Phase Four: Students analyze the data they have gathered and organized, and then test their hypothesis to postulate a possible answer to the original puzzlement.
5. Phase Five: Students are evaluated to ensure their understanding of the concept(s) in the intellectual puzzlement.

Instruction in inquiry-training begins by the teacher modeling a situation that is puzzling to the students. Such an approach, which can be called an intellectual confrontation, places students' minds in a state of disequilibrium. After the modeling of the puzzling situation, students make a hypothesis about the intellectual confrontation. During the next phase, students are provided appropriate sources in the environment. Then, students are asked to organize their data in order to provide support for their hypothesis. Next students are guided to carry out experimentation and to eliminate irrelevant information. The final phase of inquiry-training involves an analysis of organized data by the students, and the development of a conclusion that provides a possible answer to the original hypothesis that may explain the original puzzlement.

Research has provided some answers for the effects of inquiry-training. Schrenker (1976) reported that inquiry-training resulted in increased understanding of science, productivity in creative thinking, and skills for obtaining and analyzing information. Research conducted by Voss (1982) concluded that the inquiry-training strategy is effective both for elementary and secondary students.

Discovery Learning

Discovery learning emphasizes exploring, experimenting, doing research, asking questions, and seeking answers. Discovery learning was conceived on the assumption that acquisition of the relevant materials or concepts will happen during the learning activities. Bruner (1961) believes that discovery learning assists learners to take responsibility for their own learning, emphasizes higher level thinking, focuses on intrinsic rather than extrinsic motivation, and helps students remember important facts.

In discovery learning it is possible to provide no structure. However, in a great majority of teaching and learning situations, it is preferable to have some structure to the teaching activities. There are many different forms that discovery-learning techniques can take. I recommend the use of the following steps in developing lessons that are based on discovery learning:

- Identify the problem
- Formulate hypothesis
- Collect data
- Analyze data and form a conclusion.

Implications of Cognitive Theories to E-Learning

The work of Piaget and other scholars on cognitive development and children's learning had profound impact on the constructivism movement in the U.S. Two American visionaries of the 1960's who had a huge impact on the constructivism movement in teaching and educational technology were Seymour Papert and Robert Davis. Papert, who was trained by Piaget for several years, directed the LOGO project at MIT and Professor Davis, who is identified with a computer-based discovery learning pedagogical approach, directed the Plato Project at the University of Illinois.

Papert viewed computers as a tool that should be controlled by children, and its open architecture would allow children to construct their own knowledge. LOGO was invented as a programming language that allowed children to construct their own knowledge. Based on the success of the original LOGO, Microworlds as an environment in which children can explore and construct their knowledge was conceived by Papert. *Turtle Geometry* is one of the original Microworlds in which children as designers, constructors, and explorers could get to know this learning environment and restructure it or even add another Microworld to it.

Davis, on the other hand, believed that computers should control and guide the child towards constructing their own knowledge. The Plato project that was conceived by Davis used terminals with plasma panels that allowed text, graphics, animation, and audio. The ability to integrate text, graphics, animation, and audio in computers established the concept of computers as multimedia interactive textbooks. The Plato project was inspirational for educational games as well as for the development of authoring tools such as *HyperCard, HyperStudio, Director, Authorware*, and *Flash* which allowed teachers to develop their own interactive multimedia instructional units.

Both of these approaches are different from Suppes philosophy of strict steps and procedures toward rote memorization of fact and figures (See Chapter 2 for more detail). Papert and Davis both support the concept of discovery learning and inquiry training where the role of the computer is not to impose knowledge structure, but to provide the technological environments for the constructive learning process. Fortunately, the evolution of technological innovations brought about the introduction of Hypertext and authoring tools such as HTML, Flash, and QuickTime. With these new innovations in technology, it became possible to use methodologies such as simulation, educational games and hypertext to develop educational materials that were compatible with the philosophy of constructive learning, inquiry-training, and discovery learning. In what follows I will present examples that were developed by NASA's Educational Technology Teams that use emerging technologies to develop inquiry-training, hypermedia, and discovery learning in simulation.

Inquiry-Training and Hypermedia
Influential educational technology theorists such as Duffy and Jonassen (1991) became interested in constructivism. This new breed of instructional designer believed that learning and construction of knowledge rather than instruction is the focal issue. They viewed learning as a process in which children

interact with the world to construct, test, and refine their own cognitive representation of the world. Technology is viewed as a tool that allows the development of environments or educational programs in which children through interacting with its elements construct their own knowledge. Fortunately, in the early 1990's, the development of hypertext and authoring programs (e.g. *HyperCard*) collectively known as *hypermedia*, paved the way for the rise of contructivism and inquiry-training in educational technology.

With the explosion of the Web as a medium of delivery for instruction, the popularity of the contructivism movement and the inquiry-training models of teaching also took a rise in popularity. Proponents of the inquiry-training model often expressed their dislike for the traditional computer-based approach of tutorial and practice and drill. With the rise of the Web and hypermedia, the philosophy of inquiry-training was applied to technology under a variety of different terms such as project-based training, guided inquiry, inquiry-based projects, information competency, and resource-based education.

All of these different approaches to the inquiry-training process share attributes that were first proposed by Suchmann (1962). The vast majority of these methods emphasize the same attributes that can be summarized into how to find, gather, evaluate, and organize information to hypothesize a possible answer to an intellectual confrontation. In one form or the other, these steps have been used to design and develop hypermedia-based instructional materials. One of the well known educational development companies that has used these steps is Tom Snyder Production. They created a series of effective technologically based programs such as the Great Ocean Rescue and the *Great Solar Rescue.*

With the popularity of the Web, resource based instructional projects became an effective way of designing constructive e-learning environments. Today there are a number of Web sites that are devoted to inquiry-training and resource-based learning. For example, the Exploratorium Institute for Inquiry provides workshops, programs, on-line support, and an intellectual community of practice that affords science reform educators a deep and rich experience of how inquiry learning looks and feels. The URL for this Web site is

http://www.exploratorium.edu/IFI/index.html.

Another popular Web site for problem-based learning is *The Nuts and Bolts of the Big Six*, which is offered by Pac Bell under a very successful program called Knowledge Network Explorer. The URL for this Web site is

http://www.kn.pacbell.com/wired/big6/index.html

Fortunately, in recent years a huge number of hypermedia tools such as Director, Authorware and especially Flash has been developed for the Web that allow the development of a structured or guided program using the inquiry-training model. NASA has developed several successful and effective programs using the inquiry-training model and Director or Flash as development tools. One such program is Astro-Venture, which will be discussed in detail below as an example of an e-learning environment for the Web that has implemented the inquiry-training model.

NASA's Astro-Venture

Astro-Venture is an educational, multimedia Web environment in which students in grades 5-8 role-play NASA occupations as they search for and design a planet that would be habitable to humans.   This site was developed under the direction of Christina O'Guinn of the NASA Ames Educational Technology Team. *Astro-Venture* uses online multimedia activities and off-line inquiry explorations to engage students in guided inquiry aligned with Suchman's inquiry-training model. Figure 3.1 shows the main page of the *Astro-Venture* Web site.

Figure 3.1 Astro-Venture
http://astroventure.arc.nasa.gov

In *Astro-Venture*, students are first presented with the intellectual confrontation of how to design a planet and star system that would be able to meet their biological survival needs. Students hypothesize about the aspects of Earth and our star system that allow human habitation. As newly accepted members of the Astro-Venture Academy, they are informed that they will be working closely with NASA scientists who will help them in their research to better understand how the Earth meets human biological needs and, thus, the essential elements in designing a habitable planet.

Students conduct this research by engaging in multimedia training modules that allow them to change astronomical, atmospheric, geological and biological aspects of the Earth and our star system and to view the effects of these changes on Earth. By focusing on Earth, students draw on their prior knowledge that helps them to connect their new knowledge to their existing schema. Cause and effect relationships of Earth provide a concrete model from which students can observe patterns and generalize abstract results to an imagined planet. From these observations, students draw conclusions about what aspects allowed Earth to remain habitable, and they observe large themes such as the many conditions that play a role in allowing Earth to have liquid water.

Once students have generalized needed conditions of what we need for a habitable planet, they conduct further research in off-line classroom activities that also follow the inquiry model and help students to understand why we need these conditions.   These lessons follow the inquiry structure commonly referred to as the *Five E's* as follows:

1. Engage: This section draws on students' prior knowledge, builds on previous lesson concepts, introduces the purpose of the lesson and the scientific question that is the problem or intellectual confrontation they will explore.

2. Explore: Students make predictions or hypotheses in response to the scientific question and are given an activity that will help them to collect data and evidence to answer the scientific question.

3. Explain: Students reflect on the explore activity by recording their results and conclusions. They discuss these as a class or in small groups and receive feedback on their ideas. They may also engage in readings or additional demonstrations that provide further explanations of the concepts that they have explored.

4. Extend/Apply: Students are given an activity or assignment in which they demonstrate their understanding of the concept and/or apply it to another situation. Again they receive feedback on their learning.

5. Evaluate: Students are evaluated on their understanding of the concept often using rubrics. In addition, students discuss and summarize the main concepts of the lesson.

Table 3.2 shows the similarities between the phases of instruction for the inquiry-training model and the Five E's.

TABLE 3.2 Comparison

Five E's	Similarities	Inquiry-Training
Engage	Present a problem	Intellectual puzzlement
Explore	Make hypothesis	Hypothesis
Explain	Gather information	Gather data
Extend/Ap ply	Analyze and provide answer	Analyze data and postulate answer
Evaluate	Evaluation	Evaluate

These off-line activities engage students in explorations that guide them in discovery learning of concepts. For example, after gaining an understanding of the differences between solids, liquids, and gases, students hypothesize a cause for changes of matter from one state to another and design experiments to test their hypothesis. From this experimentation they discover that temperature is a vital condition for changing states of matter, and they conclude that a moderate temperature is necessary for allowing water to remain a liquid on Earth's surface at all times. Students also explore concepts such as systems as they begin to combine different variables symbolically and observe that many of the required conditions work together and cannot be isolated from others.

After students have mastered the whats and whys, they engage in multimedia mission modules that simulate how scientists might search for a planet and star system that meet these requirements using the inquiry process. Students are first asked to hypothesize the likelihood of finding a star system that meets these requirements. They then simulate the methods scientists might use to collect data on various stars and planets to deduce whether the star system meets the requirements for habitability or not. After collecting and analyzing this data, students are asked to draw conclusions in comparing their results to their initial hypothesis.

When students have a complete understanding of how the astronomical, biological, atmospheric and geological conditions of Earth meet our survival needs and why, they are ready to address the original confrontation of how to design a habitable planet. Students then engage in a multimedia activity in which they hypothesize various combinations of conditions, and test this hypothesis to see if it results in a planet that could support human habitation.

Discovery Learning and Simulation

The origin of simulation can be found in the research work of Professor Davis whose concept of an interactive textbook has evolved into discovery learning and simulation in education. The exact definition of educational simulation is hard to characterize. However, in this book, simulation is defined as presentation of an educational concept or procedure that students learn through interaction with e-learning environments. Simulation based on the above definition can be classified into two categories: conceptual or procedural teaching. There are two main differences between these two classes of simulations. First, the conceptual simulation is teaching a concept; whereas, procedure simulations show how to do something. Second, conceptual simulations do not have to be exact in reality presentation: reality presentation may be modified to allow teaching of the concept. However, procedural simulations should attempt to present reality as accurately as possible because they are concerned with showing how something is done. For example, a simulation about flying an Airplane that the goal of the simulation is to teach how to fly, the reality of the cockpit, weather, and other aspects of flying must be as accurate as possible.

In the first group, teaching a concept, the simulation generally presents or models a concept and allows the learner to explore, interact, and build something based on the concept. A very successful example of teaching a concept through simulation is the series of CDs developed by Electronic Arts (Maxim). *SimCity, SimEarth,* and *SimSafari* are examples of these types of simulations that are based on the premise that the learner can explore difficult concepts, such as building a city, and decide on what to do.

The second group of simulation generally teaches a procedure of how to do something. Procedural simulations should be presented accurately because they contain procedures that reflect reality. In recent years, procedural simulation has been used in medical and related education. In these fields it is essential to teach procedures that reflect reality. For example, a very popular procedural CD is *A.D.A.M*, that teaches anatomy and physiology. Accuracy in these simulations is critical. To have a sense of how discovery learning has been applied to procedural simulation, I will present the *Solar System Simulation* and the EngineSim that have been developed by NASA.

NASA's Solar System Simulator

NASA has developed a huge number of successful procedural simulations about flying, scientific procedures, and star systems. There are two wonderful procedural simulations in particular that I would like to present here. Figure 3.3 shows *Solar System Simulator*. This program simulates spectacular views of the solar system from whatever vantage you choose. All you have to do is to specify what you want to see, and it will create an exact simulated picture for you. The site is driven by planet databases, ring models, trajectory maps and the Yale Bright Star Catalog. It looks very cool to look at Earth on the day you were born or any other time you please. It is a site to look at the past, present and the future.

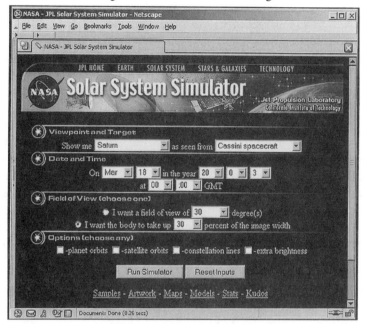

Figure 3.3 Solar System Simulator
http://space.jpl.nasa.gov/

Refection

In this chapter, I have presented a different approach to the design of multimedia learning environments. While traditional instructional design promotes a structured approach to the development of educational technology programs, the cognitive approach supports a guided learning that allows the learner to construct knowledge in the process of learning. Just like any other theoretical foundation for instructional development, there are those who support a cognitive approach to technology (Papert 1980, 1994, Jonassen, 1991), and there are also those who claim that the cognitive approach of unstructured learning is not the best use of technology (Laurillard, 1993).

Both of these two approaches are acceptable as long as they do not take a radical view. For example the radical view of the cognitive approach, that there is no structure, may prove to be futile. On the other hand, an educational technology program that is purely based on practice and drill (structured approach) may prove to be nothing more than a baby sitter in a classroom.

The cognitive approach that impacted the development of constructivist e-learning has a stronger basis in learning how to learn than the traditional structured approach. It also provides a new approach to the new attributes, such as hypertext and hypermedia that are found in modern technology. Many of the concepts that I presented in this chapter such as the inquiry-training model and the discovery-learning approach have influenced the development of successful and effective e-learning environments. Because the cognitive approach criticizes procedures, steps, and the rigid design of instructional materials, it is often much more difficult and more expensive to design and develop e-learning environments based on it. However, high cost and difficulties in design should not be the basis of what kind of effective e-learning one should develop. If your research shows that a cognitive approach is the best suited for your project, then it must be implemented. To encourage you to think about cognitive theories and constructive e-learning environments, think about how you would design a Web site or a CD-ROM about the following content areas:

- Basic math in preschool. The goal is to teach how to write One, Two,. . . . Nine.
- Pythagorean theorem in high school. How would you design a game where students would discover the Pythagorean theorem while playing the game?
- Students in an elementary school to learn about butterflies. How would you design that implementing discovery learning?
- You would like to design a Web page about AIDS for middle school students. How would you design such a Web site using the inquiry-training model?
- Study of the human brain for middle school. How would you design a procedural simulation showing brain activities?

- Eating habits for middle school. How would you design a game to encourage young people to eat appropriately?
- Gang activities and their impact on high school students. How would you design that?
- The effect of population on the Ozone layer. How would you design a conceptual simulation on the effect of population on the Ozone layer?
- Charles Darwin's theory of evolution for high school students. How would you design a game where parts of animals are given, and the students are to put the parts together to create an animal which would survive in different environments?
- Archeology procedure for high school. How would you design this using the inquiry-training model?
- Rock formation and rock identification for elementary school. How would you design this using discovery learning?
- Design an interactive Web site to teach the effect of drugs on different parts of the human body.

Chapter 4
Social Theories and E-Learning

Children are born with an innate biological propensity to learn and construct their own knowledge in relation to the impact of the environment. In Chapter Three I discussed how scholars such as Piaget (1952) identified the active role children play in construction of their own cognitive development. The scholars also emphasized the significant role the environment plays in construction of knowledge and maturation. However, although these prominent researchers did conceive of the environment as an indispensable influence on cognitive development, they also considered cognitive and psychological development as self-constructed. There needs to be a detailed explanation of internal or external mediating tools that assist self-construction of the child's cognitive development from social, cultural, and contextual factors.

There are several scholars who have provided detailed explanations of how mediating tools, such as language, modeling, and external forces can assist children to construct their own cognition. The most prominent scholar in this area is Vygotsky (1978, 1992). I shall first present Vygotsky's sociocognitive theory. Then, I shall discuss the design for e-learning environments (e.g. the Web) as an appropriate technological tool to apply Vygotsky's sociocognitive theory (1978, 1992). To achieve these goals, I shall discuss the following topics:

- Vygotsky's Sociocognitive Theory
  - Internalization of External Activities
  - The Role of Language in Cognitive Development
  - Relationship between Learning and Development
  - Knowledge Formation within the Zone of Proximal Development
- Application of Social Cognitive Theories to Models of Teaching

o   Social Inquiry Teaching Model
* Implication of Social Cognitive Theories to Design of E-Learning Environments
    o   Social Inquiry Teaching Model and the Web
    o   NASA Quest: Planetary Flight as an Example of the Social Inquiry Training Model

Vygotsky's Sociocognitive Theory

Vygotsky (1962, 1978) postulated one of the most robust and original social theories that actually explain how social factors, with language as a mediating tool, can assist in the formation of cognitive development. At age twenty-eight, he plunged into psychology and worked intensely for ten years before he died of tuberculosis in 1934. Most of his work was done in the 1920's and early 1930's. However, for political reasons the results of his research and publications did not reach the West till the 1960's.   With the original translation and publication of *Thought and Language* (1962), Vygotsky became a living theoretical force within the academic arena of the United States.

Vygotsky's *social cognitive theory* also has tremendous implications for education and the Web as a social tool. A salient feature of Vygotsky's notion is that human development and learning (e.g. social characteristics, communication styles, personality, cognitive ability, linguistic style, and academic background) originate and develop out of social and cultural interaction within what he calls the *zone of proximal development*. A brief overview of four major themes that occur in Vygotsky's works is vital to understanding the zone of proximal development. These themes are

* Internalization of external activities
* The role of language in cognitive development
* Relationship between learning and development
* Knowledge formation within the zone of proximal development

Internalization of External Activities

Internal restructuring of external social patterns is what Vygotsky refers to as *internalization*. Vygotsky (1978, 1992) has argued that a child's development cannot be understood by a study of the individual. One must also examine the external, social, and historical world in which the individual's life develops. Development is a collaborative enterprise between the members of the society and the child. Each member of the society assists the child by providing a learning environment that facilitates the child's cognitive development. This learning assistance is repeated many times during ontogenetic development and enables the child to master the cognitive, linguistic and cultural patterns of his or her environment. This notion of socially based cognitive development by Vygotsky claims that all higher human functions develop at two levels: the social plane and the psychological plane.

> Every function in the child's cultural development appears twice: first, on the social level, and later, on the individual level; first, between people (interpsychological), and then inside the child (intrapsychological). This applies equally to voluntary attention, to logical memory, and to the formation of concepts. All the higher functions originate as actual relations between human individuals. (1978, p.57)

The process, by which social patterns become psychological, is called internalization. This is not a passive transfer of external activities. Rather, children actively reorganize and restructure their internal knowledge as more external planes are introduced by an adult, more capable peers, or parents. When the process of social activities is repeated over time, children will internalize the social patterns at the psychological level and that becomes their inner perception of themselves and the world.

The Role of Language in Cognitive Development

In Vygotsky's view, internalization of inner perceptions does not occur in a vacuum. Rather, the transfer of perceptual patterns from the social to the individual level is mediated by tools of the mind. Language as a tool of the mind plays the most crucial role in the transformation of social patterns to individual psychological functions. Just as technical tools play an essential role in shaping the physical environment, language as a symbolic tool plays a corresponding role in the internal construction of knowledge or cognition, which is itself culturally and socially situated.

Human language develops during the early ages. Piaget (1926) refers to the early stages of language as egocentric speech. At first egocentric speech is used by children to solve problems. Children often talk to themselves in trying to solve simple problems; the more complicated the problem the more talking and planning.

Vygotsky argues that as children mature their egocentric speech, transforms itself into two separate, yet related tools: external and internal speech. External speech becomes a communicative tool (language), and internal speech becomes a vehicle for thinking and planning (thoughts). Vygotsky has stated:

> On the basis of these experiments my collaborators and I developed the hypothesis that children's egocentric speech should be regarded as the transitional form between external and internal speech. Functionally, egocentric speech is the basis for inner speech, while in its external form it is embedded in communicative speech. (p. 27, 1978)

Figure 4.1 reveals the metamorphosis of egocentric speech. The construction of individual psychological functions has its origins in social life, and it is mediated by the combination of internal and external speech that allows children to plan their activities prior to execution. During development, as children encounter social situations, internal speech becomes a vehicle for thinking and planning to deal with those situations. If they cannot analyze, organize, solve, or understand the situation on their own, then external speech becomes a communicative tool by means of which children are assisted in understanding socially situated situations. As these social patterns are mastered by children through self-discovery (internal speech) or guided interactive discovery (external speech), their cognition develops.

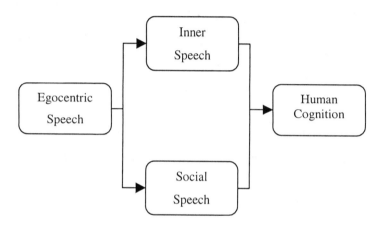

Figure 4.1 Metamorphosis of Egocentric Speech

Cognitive development, therefore, is the internalization of these social patterns; tools such as language mediate them. In the design of curriculum for education we should carefully consider the use of language as a tool to promote cognitive development and academic achievement. Exclusion of language as one of the essential tools in the design of curriculum results in inadequacies for both cognitive development and academic learning.

Relationship between Learning and Development
    One of Vygotsky's major concerns was the relationship between learning and development. He stated, "The problem encountered in the psychological analysis of teaching cannot be correctly resolved or even formulated without addressing the relationship between learning and development in school-age

children" (1978, p.79). He found Piaget's and Thorndike's explanations of the relationship between learning and development inadequate (1978).

He disagrees with Piaget who assumed that learning is separated from development and that the former is a condition for the latter. Vygotsky criticizes Piaget's notion of the relationship between learning and development by stating " that development is always a prerequisite for learning and that if a child's mental functions (intellectual operation) have not matured to the extent that he is capable of learning a particular subject, then no instruction will prove useful" (1978, p.80).

Vygotsky also criticizes the behaviorist viewpoint that learning is development. In this view (see three) learning is viewed as a series of habits. Once a new habit has been learned, development then occurs. Learning then is mastery of conditioned reflexes that provides the basis of development. Vygotsky eloquently rejects both developmental as well as behavioral views:

> ...there is a major difference in their assumption about the temporal relationship between learning and developmental processes. Theorists who hold the first view assert that developmental cycles precede learning cycles; maturation precedes learning and instruction must lag behind mental growth. For the second group of theorists, both processes occur simultaneously; learning and development coincide at all points in the same way that two identical geometrical figures coincide when superimposed. (p. 81, 1978)

He continues his discussion of the relationship between learning and development by stating that, "Although we reject all three theoretical positions discussed above, analyzing them leads us to a more adequate view of the relationship between learning and development" (p. 84, 1978). Vygotsky postulates that the relationship between learning and development is a dynamic process. He believes that instruction and learning actually causes the psychological functions that are in the process of being

developed to come to life. In other words, functions that are in
the process of maturation will mature if instruction in terms of
environmental stimuli is provided. This situation is very similar
to what happens in nature. For example, a cherry tree that has
blossomed needs an appropriate environment (warm climate,
sun, water and nutrition) to reach its full potential and produce
cherries. Without external stimuli, neither the cherry tree nor the
child will ever reach its full potential.

A child's development is a dynamic process where the
child interacts with the social cultural environment of his/her
surrounding and actively constructs his/her own knowledge.
Vygotsky calls the functions that are in the process of developing
the "buds" or "flowers" of development rather than the "fruit"
(p. 86, 1978). Instruction causes these buds to develop into
flowers. In other words, learning causes maturation of the
functions that are in an embryonic state of development.
Vygotsky concludes, "Instruction is good only when it proceeds
ahead of development" (1978). Instruction awakens and rouses
to life an entire set of functions, which will mature only if a
mentor guides it.

Knowledge Formation within the Zone of Proximal Development

Internalization of social patterns into psychological
learning occurs within the confines of what Vygotsky calls the
zone of proximal development (1978). It is within this zone that
by the use of internal tools such as language, that social
characteristics, communication styles, personality, cognitive
ability, linguistic style, and academic knowledge are transmitted
from external social activities into internal psychological
knowledge. It is also within this zone that if proper instruction
through social mediation takes place, the child's development
will shape.

Vygotsky believes that the relationship between learning
and development begins from the moment of birth and continues
during the school years and beyond. Such an incessant and
dynamic process has at least two levels that relate to
development: One level is what the child can do on her or his

own, and the second is what the child is capable of achieving if the appropriate environment and assistance are provided. In other words, the child has the potential of doing more if assisted.

Vygotsky introduced the zone of proximal development to explain the dynamic relationship between learning and development. He defines it as "the distance between the actual developmental level as determined by individual problem solving and the level of potential development as determined through problem solving under adult guidance or in collaboration with more capable peers" (1978, p. 86). Figure 4.2 shows the concept of the zone of proximal development as a recursive learning and developmental process where actual development (individual problem solving) is transformed into potential development (problem solving under adult guidance or in collaboration) with assistance from other members of the society.

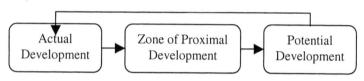

Figure 4.2 The Zone of Proximal Development

The transition from actual development to potential development is not abrupt. In fact, the progress through the zone of proximal development assumes three transitions:

- Transition occurs as the result of mediation by tools.
- Transitions follow specific phases.
- Transitions are effective when there is a shifting role or relationship between the learner and the mentor.

As already mentioned, Vygotsky argued that children restructure their own internal cognitive behavior as the result of interactions between the learner and the environment and this restructuring is mediated by tools. Vygotsky insisted on the primacy of language as a psychological tool that mediates between the learner and the environment in the process of the development of higher mental functions. However, symbolic tools can be anything including the Web.

Transfer of actual development to potential development progresses through roughly four sequential phases where there is a gradual change between the role of a mentor and the role of the learner. The role of the mentor is to provide both the content domain of knowledge and cognitive strategies. Cognitive strategies essentially have two significant contributions. First they act as organizing elements for conveying content of subject domain from the social and situational level to the intraspychological level. Second, cognitive strategies are also provided for the students to learn as an instrument of self-regulation.

The role of students in this dynamic learning environment changes as they progress through the zone of proximal development. First, the learners are passive as they rely on the modeling and presentation of the mentor on concepts of the potential development. Next, the students become passively active by collaborating with others to solve problems using such tools as language. Then, students become active and rely on their acquired knowledge to reflect on what they have learned and to seek ways for further learning. Finally, students internalize the new concept by generating cognitive strategies to transfer and use the new concept to solve problems in novel situations.

Application of Social Cognitive Theories to Models of Teaching

In more recent years, mostly because of Vygotsky's influence, constructivist teaching models have placed emphasis on the social, cultural, and contextual effect of the environment. For example, the social inquiry teaching model (Gillani, 1994), cognitive apprenticeship (Collins, Brown, & Newman, 1989), and situated cognition (Collins, Brown, & Newman, 1989) have all emphasized the importance of contextual and cultural forces. I shall limit my discussion to the social inquiry-teaching model.

Social Inquiry Teaching Model

As noted, Vygotsky (1962, 1978) postulated a sociocognitive theory that states human development and learning originates and develops out of social and cultural interaction as mediated by tools. Vygotsky's zones of proximal development can become units of instruction where socially situated settings are created. Research (Gillani, 1994) has shown that a social inquiry-teaching model that has the following sequence is an extremely effective teaching tool:

1. Students are presented with a situation where elements of an intellectual puzzlement are involved. (For example, a movie about lightning is shown, and the intellectual confrontation is to find what causes lightning.) Based upon the intellectual confrontation, students are asked to define the problem and make a hypothesis as to the nature of the problem. Students are also encouraged to develop a series of questions that may lead to a possible answer to the intellectual confrontation and to test their hypothesis.

2. Teachers and students in groups rely on each other to interact, collaborate, communicate, and react to the causes of the situation. Language here becomes an effective tool for instruction and cognitive development.

3. Students are encouraged to carry out individual research to further their learning. Students search different resources, seek scientists, teachers, and experts to gather data to narrow down their answers to the questions they formed in the pervious step. Here, students rely on sources such as the library, the Web, CDs, and other reliable resources to gather information. They isolate relevant information; organize them to provide answer(s) to the questions that would satisfy the intellectual confrontation.

4. Teacher and student groups analyze their answers to the questions and apply their learning to solve the

intellectual question and apply the result to novel situations.

Figure 4.3 shows the four phases of learning as a scaffolding progression through the zone of proximal development.

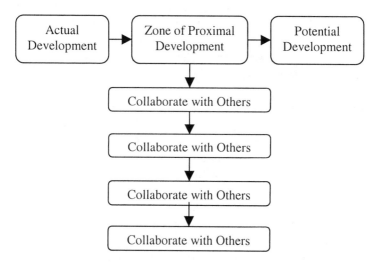

Figure 4.3 Progression through the Four Phases of the Zone of Proximal Development

In the above sequence, the learners actually progress through four phases of the zone of proximal development where there is a gradual internalization of social patterns or instructional content to internal psychological patterns (Tharp and Gallimore 1992, Gillani 1994, 1997, 1998). These phases are reliance on others, collaboration with others, self-reliance, and internalization.

The role of students in this dynamic learning environment changes from passive to collaborative to active as they progress through the zone of proximal development (Gillani 1994). During each phase the concept of scaffolding enables the learner to progress through the phases from total reliance on others, to collaboration with others, to self-reliance as support fades, and finally to internalization of the goal of the educational activities.

Implication of Social Cognitive Theories to Design of E-Learning Environments

Vygotsky's concept of social cognitive theories and the teaching models that were discussed, have been applied in several educational technology programs. In the following I will limit my dialogue to the social inquiry-teaching model for the Web, and discuss in detail its application to an exemplary educational technology developed by NASA.

Social Inquiry Teaching Model for the Web

In the teaching model based on the zone of proximal development presented by Gillani (1994), activities are not limited just between two individuals. Rather, activities involve a community of mentors who collaborate with the individual learner to achieve an educational goal. Such collaborative interaction is socially situated and the activity is distributed between the members of the community and the individual learner. The relationship between the learner and each member of the community must be well coordinated so that their roles and their responsibilities can assist the learner to effectively progress through the zone of proximal development.

Vygotsky's notion of the zone of proximal development can provide an appropriate teaching model for the Web that involves a community of mentors in a collaborative environment. The Web, as an educational tool, is a flexible multimedia communication network that can combine content presentation, interactive and collaborative communication, research for further learning, and also be a production tool for students' hands-on activities. Such a network is not limited to being between the learner and one mentor; rather, the Web is a collaborative too that can connect a community of mentors with individual learners.

The four phases of progression through the zone of proximal development (*reliance on others, collaboration with others, self-reliance*, and *internalization*) can also provide the order of instruction of a social inquiry-learning model for the Web. Such a model is socially based and learners subconsciously inquire to learn about social and academic activities. Figure 4.4 shows how such a teaching model can be applied to design of the Web as a mediating tool that guides and scaffolds the activities of the learner through each phase of instruction.

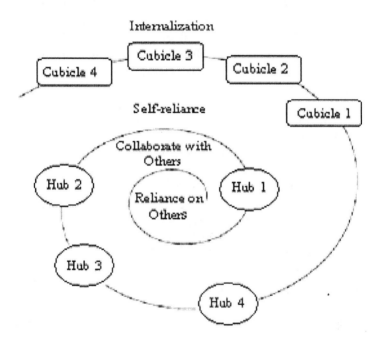

Figure 4.4 Social Inquiry Model of Teaching for the Web

The activities, as shown in Figure 4.4, are social inquiry based. Instruction begins with an intellectual confrontation and learners are then scaffold through inquiry procedures to ask essential questions, to find, gather, evaluate, and organize information, and then it fades to independent research to further learning, and finally to provide a possible answer to the intellectual confrontation where the concept has been internalized.

The Web's presentation, communication, research, and production features fit appropriately with the four phases of the zone of proximal development as well as with the syntax of the social inquiry-teaching model. In the Reliance on Others phase, the learners are passive as they rely on the mentor to model and present the intellectual puzzlement. Considerable multimedia units for the Web should be used to invoke students' prior knowledge and to generate students' interest in the concept. For example, if the educational goal of instruction is survival of animals, then a variety of graphics, video, animation, audio, and text about animals around the world should be presented. Furthermore, stories and animation about endangered species and reproduction can also spark students' interests in the survival theme of the units. Finally, during this phase a clip of endangered species, as an intellectual confrontation, could be shown, and students asked what they might do to save animals from extinction.

In the Collaboration with Others phase, each student enters a community of learning centers on the Web called Hubs (see Figure 4.4). In these Hubs students are guided to interact and collaborate with members of the community who serve as mentors. The function of each mentor is to assist students to gain more information concerning the intellectual confrontation. Each Hub would represent centers for different disciplines where teachers, professors, mentors, parents, administrators and more capable peers provide assistance for the students to gain more information in regards to the original intellectual confrontation. These centers do not necessarily have to be academic. Some of these Hubs can be learning centers where students can gain more information about cultural and personal attributes that would assist them to achieve the educational goal as defined in phase I.

Continuing with the same theme of animal survival as an example, five different areas can be designed to represent math, science, language, art, and social studies. Each of these centers could have chat rooms, forums, and video conferencing to create interactive centers where students can communicate with each other and the mentor about the survival of animals. Students are encouraged to move from one center to another to discuss animal survival from the different perspectives of different disciplines. Such interdisciplinary interaction allows the mentor and the more capable peers to assist students to gain knowledge about animals and to understand how different disciplines deal with the theme of survival. Note that these "Hubs" are not limited to academic disciplines. There are Hubs for parents, principles, peers, or anyone who can assist the learner to scaffold to the next level.

In the Self-Reliance phase, students become independent and no longer require extensive assistance from others. They search different resources on the Internet to gather data to further their learning experiences. They depend on their own knowledge to seek ways for further learning. Designers should embed learning strategies and research activities as elements of the interface for the centers I called Cubicles in the previous section (See Figure 5). These strategies should encourage students to seek out other related Web sites and resources (e.g. libraries, learning centers, universities, online courses) to further their learning. Furthermore, organizational and management software for the Web should be embedded in this phase of learning to allow students to evaluate, isolate, and organize relevant information and then hypothesize a possible answer to the original intellectual confrontation question.

Continuing with the animal survival example, links can be created to related Web sites around the globe for students to carry out research. Students could also be assigned to search different libraries or online courses to find books and related articles about animal survival, or a mentoring partnership can be created with university professors in different disciplines for students to get firsthand research information. Once students have gathered information, they can isolate the relevant information and hypothesize a possible answer to the question of animal survival.

Finally, in the Internalization phase students become comfortable implementing their newly acquired knowledge. They are now capable, without much conscious effort, to be creative and to generate solutions to problems that are similar to the concept they have mastered. For example, students can create their own Web sites about what they have internalized, or they can create online communities to generate new ideas about what they have internalized and become mentors to peers who have not yet mastered the concept. Students can also work on projects, write, or deliver interactive reports on the Web about what they have learned.

Continuing with the theme of survival as an example, students might create an interactive Web site where the endangered species is placed in an environment with all the elements that cause survival or extinction of the species. Then based on the information the students have gathered they make the Web site interactive with negative elements being reduced, and the positive elements being increased to allow survival of the species.

NASA Quest: Planetary Flight as an Example of the Social Inquiry Training Model

The National Aeronautics and Space Administration's Education Office continues to create on the Internet social learning environments that engage students in collaborative scientific investigations on-line. Many of these are illustrative of the instructional methodology involved with the social-cognitive learning theories. Following the aforementioned four phases of reliance on others, collaboration with others, self-reliance, and internalization, the NASA Quest Web site *Planetary Flight* (http://quest.nasa.gov/aero/planetary) provides opportunities for students to collaborate in the problem-solving process.

NASA Quest creates an on-line environment in which students from all over the world can interact with each other to collectively and collaboratively solve a problem. NASA Quest in conjunction with NASA researchers, scientists and engineers pose a real-world scientific problem for the students to solve. Students worldwide are grouped into teams who work collaboratively to research the important information needed to help them find the best possible solution to the problem posed. Students exchange ideas and messages via message boards and teacher e-mail. Students interact in live (and archived) Web chats and Web casts with specialists in the field that answer questions, and by posing appropriate questions of their own guide students in the problem solving process. During Web casts these specialists can offer scientific demonstrations that address the students' questions. The Web casts can also feature a virtual tour of a research facility all the while providing input that assists students in solving the problem posed. Using the on-line Q & A students can pose their own questions and later receive answers from NASA specialists in the field. Students can also access through this Web site, QuickTime movies and animations that explain scientific concepts, graphics that illustrate scientific theories, and archived interviews with experts in the field offering their research data. These Collaborative Projects from NASA Quest provide a social-cognitive model of teaching using Internet technology.

Figure 4.5 shows the main page of the *Planetary Flight* Web site.

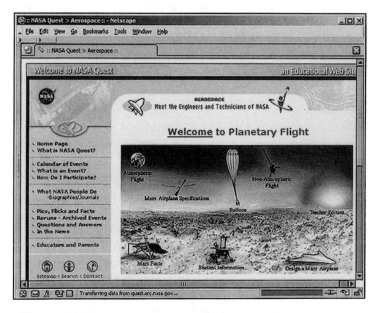

Figure 4.5 The Main Page of the Planetary Flight Web Site

Examining the main page of the NASA Quest Web site *Planetary Flight* (as shown in Figure 4.5), we find all the aforementioned on-line components contained within the four phases of reliance on others, collaboration with others, self-reliance, and internalization. Students are confronted on the main page with a landscape of Mars upon which are various icons representing diverse types of flying and land-based vehicles.

Within the Welcome button, students are encouraged to explore the Web site's aeronautical information, to interact with the Web chats and Web casts, and to apply their knowledge in designing an aircraft to fly within the Martian atmosphere. Although, at first glance, the four phases of the social inquiry-teaching model are not apparent, searching the different areas of the main page (See figure 4.5) reveals the corresponding phases of instruction for the social inquiry-teaching model. Table 4.1 shows the corresponding instructional order with the four phases of instruction in the social inquiry model.

Table 4.1 Comparison

Social Inquiry Teaching	Planetary Flight
Intellectual Confrontation	Student Information
Reliance on Others	Teachers Edition
Collaborate with Others	Events (Chat, Forum)
Self-Reliance	Individual Research
Internalization	Prototype Design of Airplane

Let's look at these phases of instruction for the *Planetary Flight* Web site in some detail. By clicking on the Students Information button, students are confronted by an aeronautical problem that is to design an airplane to fly over the surface of Mars: "Join us here at this site to learn more about Mars, its gravity and its atmosphere. Explore the differences between atmospheric and non-atmospheric flight. Learn also about the types of scientific instruments that would be used for such a data-gathering mission. Review all the information given at this Web site and through its links when considering a design for a Mars airplane. Then, apply your knowledge to design an aircraft that will fly on Mars" (http://quest.arc.nasa.gov/aero/planetary/introduction.html).

In the teacher's edition of the site that can be printed, students are further encouraged to meet the problem by accessing the following Web sites or accessing printouts from the following Web sites, and reading about the NASA announcement for a Mars aircraft to be flown in 2003. Wired News URL:

http:// www.wired.com/news/technology/0,1282,14708.00.html

This level of instruction corresponds to the reliance on others phase of the social inquiry-teaching model that was presented earlier in which students are presented with a situation where elements of an intellectual puzzlement are involved. Based upon the intellectual confrontation and molding of videos of Mars Airplane Concepts presented on the same page, students are encouraged to define the problem by asking essential question such as

- What is the gravity on Mars, and how does that affect the four forces?
- What is the composition of the atmosphere on Mars?
- What is the atmospheric pressure on Mars, and how would that affect flight?
- What are the general effects of Mars' atmosphere on flight?
- What is the effect of Mars' gravity on weight and payload?
- What is the effect of the density of Mars' air on flight?
- What is the difference in the air/atmosphere of Mars' upper atmosphere and lower atmosphere?
- Would there be a difference between Mars' upper and lower atmosphere in an airplane's ability to fly?

- How does the atmosphere of Mars affect the performance of a typical propulsion system (jet engine, propeller, rocket engine)?

In order to design the Mars plane, students are encouraged to act as aeronautical researchers. They will need to research the basics of Earth-bound aeronautics, and then see how these aeronautical principles apply in the atmosphere of Mars. Knowing how these principles act differently within the Mars atmosphere will affect ultimately the design of the aircraft. They take part in collaborating with others to gather information. In this phase, teachers and their students interact on-line in their virtual research communities to deliberate the salient questions that need answers or to discuss the important issues that need consideration. Teachers are provided with all the scientific data and information they need to know in order to guide their students along this learning path. All this instructional information is found within the Teacher's Edition. Using the Collaborative Project's bulletin board as well as their teacher's own school e-mail, students begin to form a list of information they need to acquire as well as a plan for how to acquire it. Once the plan is delineated per each participating team, their communication moves from hypothetical chatter to real research collegiality. Teachers and their students worldwide work collaboratively on-line to research and share their information as they virtually discuss how best to solve the problem of flight on Mars. This phase corresponds to Collaborating with Others in the social inquiry-teaching model where teachers and students in groups rely on each other to interact, collaborate, communicate, and react to the causes of the situation. Language here becomes an effective tool for instruction and cognitive development.

The NASA's Calendar of Events exemplifies the Collaborate with Others phase of instruction in the social inquiry teaching model. Figure 4.6 shows the Calendar of Events page for NASA Quest's *Planetary Flight*. Here students are encouraged to participate in the Chat room, Webcast, Forum, and the content area. They can actually talk to Astronauts, NASA scientists, peers, and others. Students from all over the globe can participate in the events, and get information from each other or scientists to design an airplane to fly over the surface of Mars.

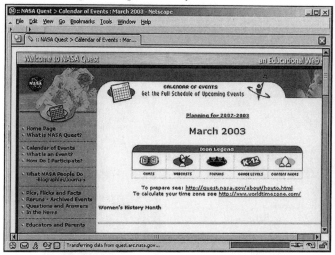

Figure 4.6 Calendars of Events Quest's Planetary Flight
http://quest.arc.nasa.gov/calendar/index.html

    In the next phase that roughly corresponds to the Self-Reliance phase of the social inquiry teaching model, the Web site encourages students to gather information from the three areas of Atmospheric Flights, Non-Atmospheric Flight, and Ballooning. For example, figure 4.7 shows the page for Atmospheric Flight. Here students can gather independent information about flight on earth. Moving on to the next phase, teachers can then motivate their students to investigate a new design in order to fly an aircraft on another planet in our solar system (such as Mercury or Venus). By following the same process and examining some of the same types of questions, students can apply what they have learned to a new planetary flight design problem that is similar, yet different. Similar in that the end result is an aircraft that can fly on another planet. Different, however, in that the atmospheric conditions on each planet are not the same; therefore, the aircraft's design needs to consider these differences.

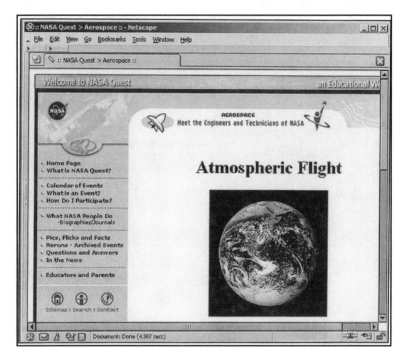

Figure 4.7 Finding Information about Atmospheric Flight

Once students have adequately researched their essential questions and the teacher believes the students are able to reflect intelligently upon their information, it is time to allow the students to actually choose prototype designs. This phase of instruction corresponds with the Internalization phase of the social inquiry teaching model where students analyze their answers to the questions, apply their learning to solve the intellectual question, and then apply the result to novel situations. They do so by accessing the Web site's section Design a Mars Airplane. Figure 4.8 shows the page in which students take an active role to design an airplane that will fly over the surface of Mars.

Figure 4.8 Design a Mars Airplane

Here students mix and match various airplane parts and structures to design a prototype. If their research has been performed thoroughly, the students should be able to eliminate the more obvious prototype designs that could not achieve successful flight on Mars. Do not allow the students to test their ideas at this time. They are to first review the selections available and discuss the remaining possibilities within their group.

As the Planetary Flight Web site of NASA Quest expands in future years, flight on planets other than Mars will be the basis of aircraft design projects. This section of the NASA Quest Web site is one of many such examples that employ social-cognitive learning theory in their development. Listed below are other examples of social-cognitive teaching models developed by NASA:

http://quest.nasa.gov/aero/planetary/welcome.html
http://quest.nasa.gov/aero/planetary/marsplane.html
http://quest.nasa.gov/aero/planetary/introduction.html
http://quest.nasa.gov/aero/planetary/atmospheric.html
http://quest.nasa.gov/aero/planetary/nonatmosphere.html
http://quest.nasa.gov/aero/planetary/atmospheric/balloon.html
http://quest.nasa.gov/aero/planetary/mars.html
http://quest.nasa.gov/aero/planetary/images.html
http://quest.nasa.gov/aero/planetary/movies.html
http://quest.nasa.gov/aero/planetary/welcome.html#events

Reflection

In more recent years, mostly because of Vygotsky's influence, constructivist teaching models have placed emphasis on the social, cultural, and contextual effect of the environment. For example, the social inquiry teaching model (Gillani, 1994), cognitive apprenticeship (Collins, Brown, & Newman, 1989), and situated cognition (Collins, Brown, & Newman, 1989) have emphasized the importance of context and cultural forces. These three social cognitive teaching models have some features in common, yet they differ in other aspects. In this chapter, the emphasis has been on the social inquiry model. However, the concepts behind cognitive apprenticeship and situated cognition also have great potential for the Web.

The cognitive apprenticeship model is based on a traditional view of transforming expert knowledge to the learner through observation, coaching, and successive approximation (Collins, 1989). The apprenticeship model is also concerned with the social context in which learning occurs. The salient feature of cultural context must be embedded in the model as well as cognitive and metacognitive strategies.

The situated cognition model that has been developed by the Cognition and Technology Group at Vanderbilt University (CTGV, 1991, 1993) emphasizes the importance of situating learning in a context in which the learner can engage in sustained exploration (Cognition & Technology Group, 1992). They emphasize that when learning occurs in isolation as separate topics, the learning remains inert. They argue that situated learning can facilitate the development of usable knowledge.

The Web, as an educational tool, is a flexible multimedia communication network that can combine content presentation with interactive and collaborative communication, do research for further learning, and be a production tool for students' hands-on activities. These wonderful aspects of the Web make it an ideal tool through which the apprenticeship model and situated cognition model can be applied to create e-learning environments that are contextual

Chapter 5
Psychological Theories and E-Learning

It is ironic that nature offers a thematic and integrated presentation of the natural environment to the human brain (which functions on an integrated basis), yet our educational system is based on a disciplinary and fragmented approach. We break human knowledge into disciplines and force our students to study math during first period, English the second, and so on. Yet when students enter the job market, nobody expects them to do math only from 8:30 till 9:25. Rather, the expectation for our graduates is to solve problems by using an integrated approach. Research (Caine and Caine, 1992, Bransford, J., et al., 1999) has clearly shown that both children and experts learn better and solve problems better with an integrated thematic approach. This chapter provides evidence from research on human memory and psychological theories that supports the goals of integrated thematic multimedia learning environments. To achieve these goals, I shall discuss the following topics:

- Psychological Theories and the Thematic Nature of Development
  - Characteristics of Expert's Knowledge Organization
  - Erikson's Theory of Psychological Development
  - Types of Human Memory as They Relate to the Integrated Structure of Knowledge
- Application of Psychological Theories to Models of Teaching
- Implication of Psychological Theories to Integrated Thematic E-Learning Environments
  - Overview of the NASA SCIence Files
    - Select Unifying Themes
    - Develop Intellectual Confrontations Based on the Theme
    - Decide the Interdisciplinary Possibilities

- Determine the Activities and the Sequence of Problem-Based Learning
- Student Provides Possible Answer(s)

Psychological Theories and the Thematic Nature of Development

Today, there is a mind shift in business communities, in scientific endeavors, in educational views, in psychology, in technology, and in international relationships from seeing parts to seeing wholes. This approach has been termed systems thinking. It looks at "patterns of change rather than snapshots" (Senge, 1990, p. 68). This new way of thinking was first used by biologists, and was later supported by research in ecology and psychology. Essentially, systems thinking emphasizes thinking in terms of connectedness, relationship, and context (Capra, 1996). The essence of systems thinking involves a mind shift from parts to the whole and to learning the relationship among the parts within different contexts.

One of the most challenging aspects of e-learning in the twenty-first century will be to design instruction that promotes the ability of the students to see the whole and the relationship among its parts. To achieve this goal, new teaching models that adhere to the principles of systems theory must be formulated for the design of e-learning environments. Research in education (Kovalik, 1994) has provided the theoretical foundation for the exploration of teaching models that resemble the philosophy of systems theory in terms of the integrated thematic knowledge structure, connectedness, relationship, and context.

There is ample evidence from expert learning and developmental theory studies to support the claim that meaningful learning occurs in accordance with existing themes and integrated knowledge structures. In what follows, I shall first review some of the findings from research about the expert's ability to learn according to themes and concepts. Second, I shall describe how psychological development also occurs according to different themes at different stages of life. Finally, I shall provide evidence that teaching models should be integrated and be based on the psychological themes that are most appropriate for different stages of psychological development.

Characteristics of Expert's Knowledge Organization

Experts are those individuals who have organized their knowledge structure according to some core concepts. A novice, on the other hand, simply memorizes new information and attempts to encode it into long-term memory without much regard for its organization. The difference between the ways an expert and a novice learn to organize information becomes apparent when it comes to retrieval and problem solving. Experts are able to solve problems quickly because they have a system and a set of procedures for dealing with the problems of the field. An expert can easily retrieve relevant information to solve the problem at hand; whereas, the novice attempts in vain to use a variety of approaches to solve the problem. In other words, experts have achieved meaningful knowledge structures that are based on core themes and novices have not.

The way information is organized according to specific themes or concepts by experts is seen in all academic disciplines. In physics, for example, when experts are asked which approach they take to solve a problem, they mention a major law or concept in physics (Chi et al., 1981). Other research shows that novice learners in physics generally attempt to describe the problem in terms of equations they might use (Larkin, 1981, 1983).

Chi et al., (1982) have also shown that in representing a web-like structure for an incline plane, the novice schema is more concerned with surface knowledge; whereas, the webbing for the expert is connected to the concepts of an incline plane. These types of studies that reveal the way experts organize information is not limited to hard sciences. In social studies, it has been shown that experts also organize their problem solving according to larger concepts and themes (Bruner, 1960 and Voss, et al., 1984).

The main question, then, is what are these themes in specific disciplines that experts possess? More importantly, if we find these themes, can we then base our instructional design process on them so that students can learn the way experts do? In an attempt to find answers to these questions, I shall discuss Erikson' s theory of psychological development in which he deals with some of these questions.

Erikson' s Theory of Psychological Development

To fully understand Erik Erikson's contribution to learning and to better appreciate his contributions to educational planning, it is vital to consider Anna Freud's influence upon his research and work. Anna Freud (1946), Sigmund Freud's daughter, was particularly interested in adolescence. She considered this period as a time full of anxiety and stress because adolescents are attempting to adjust their personalities and psychic needs after the physical changes that occur during this period. Anna Freud (1946) popularized the notion that adolescence is a period that includes rapid mood fluctuation with enormous uncertainty about self.

According to Anna Freud (1946), the identity crisis, the mood shifts, and the contrasting notions that are typical of adolescence are the direct result of an imbalance between the id and ego. The id represents impulses like sexual drives that are developing in adolescents, and the ego represents the reality of the social environment. Therefore, adolescents are constantly struggling to satisfy inner impulses, such as sexual drive and its consequence of pregnancy, to that which is morally or socially acceptable. To regain psychological balance, the adolescent must find a balance between the wishes of the id and the demands of the ego. Such is the nature of the identity crisis that adolescents encounter during this period. Its ramifications overshadow their behavior, their relationships, and all other elements that constitute the adolescent. The result is that adolescence becomes a period that is marked by contrast, moodiness, rebellion, submissiveness, and goodness. The contrasts, while not appreciated by parents and teachers, are actually a sign of normal growth during adolescence. What is significant about Anna Freud's explanation of adolescence is that teenagers subconsciously become obsessed with the theme of self-identity.

Such a theme drives their lives, and everything they do is organized according to this self-identity theme.

Eric Erikson was invited by Anna Freud to join her in Vienna. Erikson was influenced by Anna Freud's perspective of adolescence that included the theme of identity crisis. He was also influenced by Sigmund Freud's theory of psychosexual stages. In fact, in his classic work *Childhood and Society* (1950), where Erikson posited a model for the developmental stages of life, one can detect the influence of both Anna and Sigmund Freud. Erikson's theory differs from Sigmund Freud's stage theory in that it is developmentally, contextually, and thematically based. It is developmental because he has delineated eight major crises over the course of life that determine personal developmental stages. It is contextual because the theory defines these eight stages and major conflicts between self and the social pressure that one has to resolve before successfully moving into the next stage. The theory is thematic because at different stages the growing child becomes concerned with specific subconscious themes.

To Erikson, physical growth follows a biological timetable: "Anything that grows has a ground plan . . . and out of this ground plan parts arise. Each part having its time of special ascendancy, until all parts have arisen to form a functioning whole" (Erikson, 1959, p52). This phenomenon is called physical epigenesis, which is universal and has nothing to do with race or nationality. There is also such a thing as universal cognitive epigenesis (Piaget, 1952). According to Piaget, human beings go through four stages of cognitive development (See Chapter 3). In addition to physical and cognitive epigenesis, there is such a thing as social epigenesis, which may be different in different cultures. Erikson (1950) believed that because we are social animals, society has also evolved certain social orders, roles, and demands that are parallel with physical growth. For example, when a child achieves control of his muscle movement, we then expect him to explore his surroundings under parental guidance; also, when a child has command of his language and is capable of taking care of rudimentary tasks, society expects him to attend school. Both physical and social epigenetic principles mature at different stages.

The interaction between physical, cognitive, and social growth during maturation in each stage of life creates a sequence of developmental crises that become central to the human's growth. These crises are driven by specific themes that are by nature contradictory. Each stage has its own contradictory theme that acts as the driving force for children to resolve and organize their own psychological development. Table 5.1 represents the eight stages of development that have been posited by Erikson.

Table 5.1 Stages of Psychological Development

Stage	Age	Central Thematic Conflict
1	Infancy	Trust versus mistrust
2	Toddlerhood	Autonomy versus shame and doubt
3	Early childhood	Initiative versus guilt
4	Middle childhood	Industry versus inferiority
5	Adolescence	Identity versus identity confusion
6	Young adulthood	Intimacy versus isolation
7	Adulthood	Generativity versus stagnation
8	Aging	Ego integrity versus despair

According to Erikson (1950), each stage of psychological development represents a major psychological crisis that one faces in life. Depending on the manner in which the crisis is resolved, one's identity is formed. Such resolutions, according to Erikson, provide the basis for the development of a conflict or dilemma for the next stage of development. In other words, each stage affects the next stage. Unsuccessful resolution of a stage may negatively affect the development of later stages in life.

The first stage occurs during infancy in which the infant is helpless and seeks the same comfort and security as in the mother's uterus. The psychological crisis that must be resolved during this period is based on the contradictory themes of Trust versus Mistrust. Everything the child internalizes during this stage is organized according to these two core concepts.

Having mastered the first stage, the child enters the next stage that deals with the themes of Autonomy versus Shame and Doubt. These two contradictory themes become central to children's psychological growth. For the first time, the environment demands that the child perform tasks independently. Successful accomplishment of these tasks with appropriate parental support gives the child a sense of autonomy. However, a child who is not encouraged to perform independent tasks and is humiliated for her/his lapses develops a sense of shame and doubt.

The next stage of development focuses on the themes of Initiative versus Guilt. According to Erikson, the child begins to explore the environment and develops a sense of taking initiatives. A feeling of guilt sets in when the child's initiatives are constantly curtailed by the caregiver or when the initiatives taken by the child exceed his/her limits.

The fourth stage is concerned with the concepts of Industry versus Inferiority. The major theme of the fourth stage is that children strive to master what they are doing. To build a sense of competence in this stage affects the ability of the individuals to have success in their task. Developing a sense of inferiority by not being able to complete a given task advances a sense of incompetence in children that will be exhibited later in life as an inability to take up responsibility. Within this stage, the child also begins to move from a parent-centered world to a peer-centered world where peers and friends have a major social influence on the child who is just beginning to enter the stage of middle childhood or young adolescence. Depending on the kind of support the young adolescent gets during this stage from parents and teachers for social as well as academic tasks, the young adolescent can resolve the dilemma of this stage and successfully enter the young adolescent stage.

The fifth stage (between ages 11 to 18) becomes concerned with the themes of Identity versus Identity Confusion. The search to find who they are, the need to be independent, and peer acceptance become central themes during this stage.

Students at the early phases of this stage become confused while trying to resolve their conflicting feelings about themselves. While students at this stage try to develop a sense of dependence, they are also obsessed with being independent of their parents and close relatives. These students search for role models and are greatly influenced by what their peers have to say about all aspects of life.

The many physical changes and a changing social environment present new psychosocial crises that require learners to develop a new sense of self. Primary issues are youngsters' search for a role identity and their concern with how they appear in the eyes of others as compared to what they feel they are. In their search for an identity, many learners during this stage begin to adopt idols, ideas, and heroes. Also, cliques can be remarkably clannish and cruel in the exclusion of others (Erikson, 1963) in this stage.

The next three stages in Erikson's developmental theory are concerned with development in adulthood. This period starts at about eighteen and extends into old age. According to Erikson, an individual who is around twenty years old begins to be concerned with the theme of Intimacy versus Isolation, which generally results in marriage or a long lasting sexual union. In the next stage, individuals become concerned with being Generativity versus Stagnation to improve themselves and the society in which they live. Finally, the last stage is concerned with the concept of Ego Integrity versus Despair. If one successfully resolves all the crises or conflicts in life, then that individual looks back and develops a sense of ego satisfaction. On the other hand, if resolutions were unsuccessful in one or more stages of development, a feeling of despair or incompetence arises in one's ego.

The universal themes that have been posited by Erikson are the core concepts around which we organize information that we encounter during different stages. The author's research and his work with students in K-16 indicate that, in addition to Erikson's universal themes, there are other universal and personal themes with which students are subconsciously concerned with during maturation (Gillani, 1998). We can call these themes *Academic Unifying Themes*. Table (5.2) shows some of these themes.

Table 5.2 Academic Unifying Themes

Unifying Themes Math	Unifying Themes Language Arts	Unifying Themes Science	Unifying Themes Social Sciences	Unifying Themes Art
Proportion	Preserva-tion	Energy	Unity	Balance
Patterns	Change	Evolution	Diversity	Symmetry
Generali-zation	Survival	Change	Inter-action	Direction
Depend-ence	Downfall	Patterns	Change	Form
Judgment	Strive	Structure	Survival	Proportion
Preserva-tion	Love	Stability	Inter-relation	Unity
Variations	Sacrifice	Reaction	Diversity	Change
Change	Conflict	Action		Patterns

These Academic Unifying Themes, very similar to the themes that experts unconsciously possess, can be the driving force behind curriculum design that would allow students to organize academic information. These unifying themes can also tie together academic areas and help us design and develop interdisciplinary courses. The most significant attribute of curriculum that is based on personal themes is that they attract students and allow them to achieve deeper or more meaningful learning.

Types of Human Memory as They Relate to the Integrated Structure of Knowledge

O'Keefe and Nadal (1978) conducted research both on animals and human beings to explain types of memories that are based on the hierarchical and interconnected nature of memory in which parts are integral pieces of the whole. They discovered two types of memory that they called taxon and locale.

Taxon memory is concerned with facts and figures and depends on rote memorization. Taxon memory, according to O'Keefe and Nadal, depends on rehearsal that allows information to be stored in the long-term memory from the short-term memory. This type of memory is like memorizing the capitals of countries, basic skills in mathematics, and chemical symbols. Because it is non-contextual and not integrated with prior knowledge, the retrieval of this type of memory is difficult when it is needed for problem solving. Furthermore, as a general rule, this type of memory must be used on a consistent basis to be remembered. If it is not used, its retrieval becomes very difficult to the point of forgetting.

Locale memory is a natural memory that is biologically driven by the limbic system. According to O'Keefe and Nadal, locale memory is contextual and situational. The hippocampus in our limbic system creates a spatial and contextual map of the environmental input. These maps are continuously reconstructed in our memory as new information is combined with prior information. The concept of locale memory is very similar to Piaget's (1952) concept of schema (See Chapter 3). Children come into any new learning environment with their own schemata that are representative of their patterns of life experiences and prior knowledge. A number of researchers (Anderson & Pearson, 1984; Piaget, 1952) have posited that schemata are the building blocks of intellectual development. During cognitive development, children's schemata are constantly restructured as they encounter new patterns in their learning experiences.

Locale memory that represents maps of environmental input becomes integrated into other locale memory, thus creating a much larger hierarchical memory that represents human knowledge structures. Within such interconnected hierarchical memory, everything is somehow connected with everything else; therefore, one cannot break down information into smaller pieces and present it to students and then expect them to put the pieces together to understand the whole. We fail to teach our students that the essential properties of the whole, and their connection to a body of information cannot be understood in terms of the properties of its parts.

Application of Psychological Theories to Models of Teaching

We have become accustomed to breaking down human knowledge into disciplines and encouraging our students to master each discipline separately. The most significant reason for disciplinary education was the idea of specializing in different disciplines. Knowledge in these disciplines is presented separately without any attempt to understand how the human brain processes information. As we have seen in this chapter, research clearly shows that the human brain functions on an interdisciplinary basis in which the relationships and connectedness of disciplines are just as important as the disciplines themselves.

The intention is not to completely dismiss a disciplinary approach to education. After all, disciplinary education has been used successfully for many years. There are a number of advantages in using a disciplinary approach. Among them are providing specialized skill, efficiency, availability of curriculum, tests, and supplementary instructional materials. However, as we have discussed, human memory such as taxon and locale functions both on a disciplinary as well as interdisciplinary or integrated approach. What is needed are complementary approaches in which disciplines are embedded into an interdisciplinary approach. Such an approach is possible if we use themes as the glue to connect disciplines together to create an interdisciplinary approach. As shown in Figure 5.1, there are four stages in the development of a thematic interdisciplinary teaching model:

- Select unifying themes
- Develop intellectual confrontations based on the theme
- Determine the activities and the sequence for problem-based learning for each discipline
- Student provides possible answer(s)

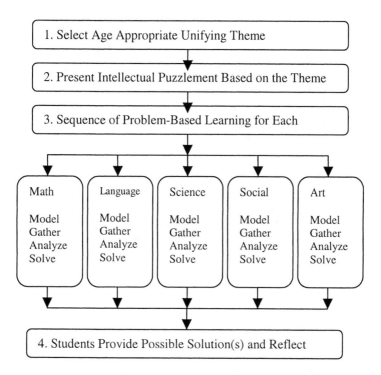

Figure 5.1 A Thematic Interdisciplinary Teaching Model

The model begins by confronting the learners with an intellectual confrontation, which can be presented through multimedia, verbally, video or by other means. The purpose is to place the student's mind in a state of inquiry. Such a state would naturally prompt the learner to investigate and solve the mystery behind the intellectual confrontation.

As the students become interested, they generally are grouped into dyads or triads. The size of the groups depends on the problem and the classroom environment. Members of each group will be organized to have select roles and responsibilities for the investigation into the intellectual confrontation. Roles of the members include:

- Principal Investigator: Coordinates all team activities.
- Reporter: Records all observations and responses of the students, and reports the final product to the audience.
- Technical: Central team member navigates the site and downloads and prints needed materials.
- Materials Manager: Gathers and returns supplies for experiments and hands-on activities.

As the students investigate the problem and write a problem statement, they develop two lists: What do we know? and What do we need to know? Based on the discrepancy between these two lists, they begin their investigation and gather information to provide a possible solution for the intellectual confrontation. They organize and analyze the information they have gathered and report their results. Finally, the group proposes its solution(s) in terms of the original intellectual confrontation and reports the findings to the teacher.

Implication of Psychological Theories to Integrated Thematic E-Learning Environments

The teaching model presented in Figure 5.1 is ideal for Web-based e-learning environments because it can be used to engage students in online investigation. The model is generally referred to as *Problem-Based Learning (PBL)*, which is based on several constructivist theories that were discussed in the previous chapters. Educational Web sites or CD-ROMs based on PBL could present students with an intellectual confrontation; then, students are grouped to analyze the problem, research, discuss, and produce tentative explanations or solutions using technology as a tool to achieve their goals and objectives.

There are numerous CD-ROMs and Web sites that have implemented PBL techniques for educational purposes. For example, *The Great Ocean Rescue*, produced by Tom Snyder Productions is a cooperative, thematic, and interdisciplinary learning CD-ROM package, in which students face four intellectual confrontations for each rescue mission. Through investigative methods, students assume the roles of scientists in ecosystems, earth and environmental science, and a host of other disciplines to rescue endangered species. The underlying theme that brings these disciplines together is preservation, which is ideal for grades, 5-8, and for which the CD-ROM was designed. According to the information provided on the Web site for Tom Snyder Productions: "In addition to these exciting missions, the CD-ROM also contains a fantastic library of over 85 short movies and stills, each tied to a comprehensive lesson plan in the Teacher's Guide. Open up the world of the oceans as never before and turn your students into hands-on scientists and interdisciplinary problem solvers." (http://www.tomsnyder.com)

There are a number of Web sites that are devoted to PBL. For example, the Samford University Center for Problem-Based Learning (http://www.samford.edu/pbl.) has five schools that are participating in their efforts to redesign the core areas of their undergraduate curriculum to include problem-based learning. These schools are Arts and Sciences, Business, Education, Nursing, and Pharmacy. Another great example of a Web site that is devoted to PBL is the Jason Project (http://www.jasonproject.org/). This project is an interdisciplinary learning environment that uses a variety of disciplines (e.g. science, math, social studies, and English) to broaden the learning experience through investigation.

NASA has carried out one of the most successful implementations of the PBL teaching model. Through numerous collaborations, NASA has been able to develop several successful PBL Web sites that are very similar to the teaching model and research that has been discussed in this chapter. The following are just a few examples of successful Web sites that have been developed by NASA through collaboration with others:

- *NASA SCIence Files*
- http://scifiles.larc.nasa.gov/treehouse.html
- *Signals of Spring*:
- http://www.signalsofspring.com/
- *Exploring the Environment*:

- www.cotf.edu/etc
- *Astronomy Village: Investigating the Solar System*: www.cet.edu/av2
- *Global Perspectives*:
- www.cet.edu/earthinfo
- *International Space Station*
- www.cotf.edu/iss

I will limit the discussion of how an interdisciplinary thematic PBL teaching model was applied by NASA to *NASA* SCIence. This exemplary e-learning environment was developed under the direction of Dr. Thomas E. Pinelli. The Page Curators for this site are Shannon Ricles, and Kevin Sparks.

Overview of The NASA SCIence Files
Figure 5.2 shows the main page of The *NASA SCIence Files* Web site.

Figure 5.2 NASA SCIence Files
http://scifiles.larc.nasa.gov/treehouse.html

According to the description provided on the site, the *NASA SCIence Files* is a series of instructional programs consisting of broadcast, print, and online elements that emphasize standards-based instruction, Problem-Based Learning, and science as inquiry. The series seeks to motivate students in grades 3-5 to become critical thinkers and active problem solvers. Each episode includes a video, an educator's guide, and online activities.

The Web site provides the following brief description of the episodes that are currently available on the Web site:

Season 2000-2001

The Case of the Unknown Stink: The tree house detectives try to find the source of an unpleasant odor that is invading the surrounding neighborhoods. To determine the source of the stink, the detectives use the scientific method and learn about the sense of smell. They also learn how NASA's Atmospheric Science research can help solve the case.

The Case of the Barking Dogs: The tree house detectives accept the challenge of determining why dogs in the surrounding neighborhoods have unexpectedly started barking early in the morning and late at night. While investigating the mystery, the detectives learn about sound: what it is, how it is transmitted, and how people and animals hear.

The Case of the Electrical Mystery: The tree house detectives notice the power has gone out in all the houses on their block, yet the electricity in their tree house is still on. Using scientific inquiry, they discover the cause of the outage while learning about electricity and how it is generated. They also learn about electrical currents, circuits, and distribution.

The Case of the Challenging Flight: The tree house detectives enter a contest to create an egg carton plane. While designing their plane, the detectives learn about the four forces of flight (lift, thrust, drag, and gravity), all in an attempt to build an "egg-tra-ordinary" flying machine.

The Case of the Mysterious Red Light: Have you ever seen an unusually bright red sunrise or sunset and wondered why its color was so intense? That's exactly what happens in *The Case of the Mysterious Red Light* as the tree house detectives accept the challenge of trying to find the source of the red light.

The Case of the "Wright" Invention: Travel back in time with the tree house detectives to learn about the process of invention from two of the greatest inventors of all time, Orville and Wilbur Wright. As the tree house detectives try to create their own invention, they get expert help from the Wright brothers, NASA researchers, and other experts in the community.

The Case of the Inhabitable Habitat: In *The Case of the Inhabitable Habitat*, the tree house detectives accept the challenge of designing a habitat that can sustain life on Mars. In order to design an award winning habitat, the tree house detectives decide that they must first learn more about the planet Mars and the various habitats found here on Earth.

The Case of the Phenomenal Weather: Join the tree house detectives as they plan a trip to the Caribbean and encounter problems trying to predict the weather. In this case, the tree house detectives will learn about violent storms such as hurricanes and tornadoes, weather fronts, global wind patterns, and climates. While solving the case, they will discover that predicting the weather is not predictable at all!

I will discuss the episode called *The Case of the Mysterious Red Light* according to the five stages in the development of a thematic interdisciplinary teaching model as follows:

- Select unifying themes
- Develop intellectual confrontations based on the theme
- Decide the interdisciplinary possibilities
- Determine the activities and the sequence of problem-based learning
- Student provides possible answer(s)

Selecting Unifying Themes

The development of a thematic interdisciplinary PBL teaching model should begin by determining a unifying theme. Unifying themes tie together subliminal concerns of the student and the content being presented. These unifying themes must be based on the concept of epigenetic universal themes (See Table 5.1 Stages of Psychological Development and Table 5.2 Academic Unifying Themes). The universal themes that have been posited by Erikson should be the core concepts around which we organize information to present to the learners.

Furthermore, these unifying themes also function as a nexus to bring together the principles of different disciplines for several content areas. For example, if the unifying theme for the whole curriculum is Preservation, then the same theme will be used to present the instructional materials for different disciplines such as mathematics, the sciences, and language arts. In this fashion, the disciplines are connected and the theme acts as the glue that provides the connectedness of the instructional materials.

In most cases, shallow and inappropriate themes like music are chosen for thematic instruction because the instructional designer thinks that teenagers like music. Creating themes around which instruction and curriculum are developed is not a superficial process. There are several important aspects of theme selection that curriculum developers should consider. Themes are age specific; themes have subcomponents.

One of the most important aspects of selecting and using unifying themes is to remember that they are age specific. To select the themes that are age appropriate, we should refer to the psychological stages that Erikson (1950) posited. During each stage of life children and adults are concerned with specific themes. For example, the theme of Identity versus Identity Confusion is most appropriate for adolescents.

The second important aspect of theme selection is that themes that are age appropriate have subthemes. The main themes can be viewed as having the ability to allow students to mature psychologically as well as the ability to guide instruction for a long period of time. The main themes such as the ones Erikson postulated are used to guide curriculum, but their main functions are to allow students to positively resolve their internal conflict to develop to the next stage of psychological development. For example, the theme for Industry versus

Inferiority is the overriding theme for the Middle Childhood stage of development. This theme should be selected to be the guiding principle for months of instruction. However, these age appropriate main themes have subthemes. For example, the unifying themes of Identity versus Identity Confusion for adolescents may have such subthemes as change, dependence, preservation, judgment, fairness, patterns, and survival, with which most adolescents are very much concerned.

One of the episodes of this Web site is *The Case of the Mysterious Red Light*. NASA has developed this effective episode as a thematic interdisciplinary PBL program using age appropriate themes to support the instructional goals. On pages 6 and 7 of the Educator's Guide, they clearly specify that they are satisfying the following recommended unifying concepts for grades K-4 and K-5 as shown in Table 5.3.

Table 5.3 National Science Standards (Grade K-4 and K-5)

National Science Standards (Grades K - 4) and (K-5)				
Unifying Concepts and Processes	1	2	3	4
Systems, orders, and organization	*	*	*	*
Evidence, models, and explanations	*	*	*	*
Change, constancy, and measurement	*	*	*	*
Evolution and equilibrium			*	
Form and function			*	

Develop Intellectual Confrontations Based on the Theme

The next step in developing a thematic interdisciplinary PBL is to create an appropriate intellectual confrontation that is based on the unifying themes. Providing an intellectual confrontation or an academic problem as the initial step of a PBL lesson is an excellent way to provide internal motivation for the students to begin the process of investigation that will provide a possible solution or explanation for the problem at hand. The intellectual confrontation is usually presented in terms of a text description, short digitized video, animation, or audio. NASA uses a novel approach to the intellectual confrontation. They provide a video series that is first broadcast by many of the PBS affiliates throughout the U.S. If one misses the first broadcast, the video of the episode can be obtained from the local Educators Resource Center. The video can also be purchased for a minimal fee from NASA's Central Operation of Resources for Educators (CORE).

(http://catalog.core.nasa.gov/core.nsf/item/099.32-02v).

The intellectual confrontation for *The Case of the Mysterious Red Light* is also revealed on the Web site: "Each day, for no apparent reason, the morning and evening sky blazes with a brilliant deep red color." Students are invited to join the tree house detectives as they try to discover what phenomena could be causing the bright red sunrises and sunsets.

(http://scifiles.larc.nasa.gov/educators/index.html).

Decide the Interdisciplinary Possibilities
The main goal of an interdisciplinary model is to bring together the disciplines' perspectives and focus on the investigation of the intellectual confrontation or the driving theme. In an interdisciplinary thematic curriculum, the designers must also brainstorm about the most suitable disciplines that need to be included in the entire curriculum, and they must be brought together through the central theme. To encourage the exploration of the theme from all disciplines involved, the designers must use webbing as an instrument to organize the disciplines and discussion. During the actual discussion of which disciplines are important and how the theme should be used, criticism should be ruled out and a quantity of ideas should be elicited. These fresh ideas should be combined and evaluated. Figure 5.3 shows how webbing assists the designers to decide on which disciplines should be involved, and how the theme is the central focus or the glue that brings these disciplines together.

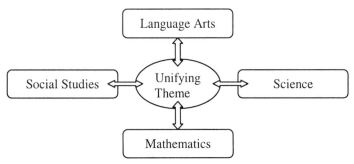

Figure 5.3 Use of Webbing for a Thematic Interdisciplinary Design

To illustrate this webbing, let us look at Figure 5.4, which shows the disciplines that are involved in the *The Case of the Mysterious Red Light*:

- Math - Numbers and Operations; Measurement; Problem Solving; Representation
- Science - Unifying Concepts and Processing; Science and Inquiry; Physical Science; Earth and Space Science; Science and Technology; Science in Personal and Social Perspective
- Technology - Basic Operations and Concepts; Social, Ethical, and Human Issues; Technology Productivity Tools; Technology Communication Tools; Technology Research Tools; Technology Problem-Solving and Decision-Making Tools
- Geography - The World in Spatial Terms; Places and Regions; Physical Systems; Environment and Society; Uses of Geography
- NASA Enterprise - Aerospace Technology; Earth Science

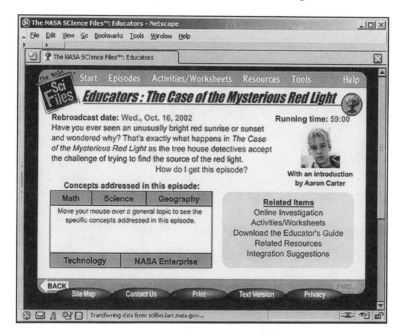

Figure 5.4 A Thematic Interdisciplinary Approach

Although it is not shown in Figure 5.4, in the episode of *The Case of the Mysterious Red Light,* students are encouraged to choose one of the following professional roles in a specific discipline to investigate the mystery: meteorologist, atmospheric scientist, geologist, and physicist.

It is essential to mention that just as the entire curriculum is based on an interdisciplinary concept, each discipline is also considered part of a bigger unit. For example, as illustrated in Figure 5.5, the science curriculum is composed of seven different strands such as earth science, physical science, life science, scientific thinking, ethics of science, research, and scientific progress. All of these strands are guided by the same unifying subtheme that is related to the main theme. In other words, different strands in each discipline are not taught in isolation. All the complimentary strands in each discipline are part of the bigger unit that is guided by the subtheme.

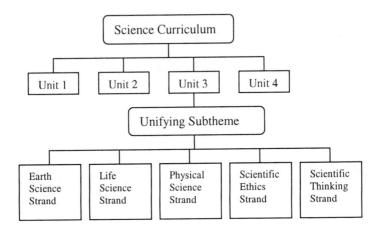

Figure 5.5 Interdisciplinary Science Curriculum

The interdisciplinary concept in which each discipline is also considered part of a bigger unit applies to all other disciplines as well as to science. For example Figure 5.6 shows that the mathematics discipline is composed of six different strands such as functions, algebra, geometry, statistics, numbers, and measurement. All these strands are guided by one unifying subtheme that is related to the main theme. In other words, just as in the science curriculum, mathematic strands are not taught in isolation. All the complimentary strands in mathematics are taught simultaneously, and they are considered to be holistic rather than isolated strands. The guiding factor that brings these strands together is the unifying subtheme.

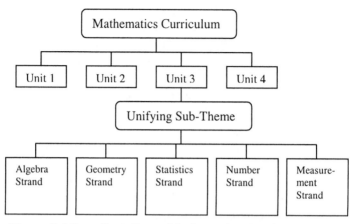

Figure 5.6 Interdisciplinary Mathematics Curriculum

Determine the Activities and the Sequence of Problem-Based Learning

The activities in a Problem-Based Learning teaching model are guided by the subthemes that are related to the main themes as discussed in the previous section. For example, in middle school and high school, where instruction and curriculum are designed for adolescents, the main theme is Identity versus Identity Confusion. However, the subthemes for this stage of psychological development are change, patterns, judgment, preservation, dependence, independence, survival, conflict, self-discovery, unity, diversity, and hierarchy. These subthemes are the organizing concepts around which the sequence and the activities of disciplinary instruction are developed. It must be emphasized that the relationship between the subtheme and the main theme is the overriding guiding organization both for psychological development as well as for the organization of instructional materials.

The sequence of activities in the teaching model for each discipline, as described above, follows the PBL teaching model that was presented in Figure 5.1. According to Finkle and Torp (1995), "problem-based learning is a curriculum development and instructional system that simultaneously develops both problem-solving strategies and a disciplinary knowledge basis and skills by placing students in the active role of problem solvers confronted with an ill-structured problem that mirrors real-world problems" (p.1). This sequence of activities for the PBL teaching model includes the following:

- Present the Intellectual Confrontation.
- Understand the Problem:
  - o List what is known. The list may include information based on the learners' prior knowledge.
  - o List what is needed. This list will guide the students to conduct a search.
- Gather Information. Learners list actions to be taken based on the list what is needed. These actions will include questioning an expert, searching on-line, in the library, in the lab, and other resources.
- Analyze Information. Formulate and test tentative hypotheses based on the information that is gathered.
- Present the Solution. Students should communicate their findings and make recommendations. Communication may be done online or by using some technology to present and support the solution.

There are variations in the implementation of the sequence of activities for PBL teaching that was presented previously. For example, the wording that was adapted by the developers of the *NASA SCIence Files* is slightly different than what has been presented here. However, what is essential is that they all follow the steps of presenting the problem, understanding the problem, gathering information, analyzing information, and providing a solution. Figure 5.7 illustrates the sequence of PBL for *The Case of the Mysterious Red Light*. It should be mentioned that other episodes of The *NASA SCIence Files* follow the exact sequence for PBL.

Figure 5.7 Sequence for PBL Activities for The Case of the
Mysterious Red Light

The menu at the bottom of Figure 5.7 contains seven
buttons that include Folder, Books, Beaker, Notebook, Monitor,
Graduation Cap, and Character. Respectively, the functions of
these buttons are Case Intro, Research Rack, Dr. D's Lab,
Problem Solving Tools, Media Zone, Expert Corner, and Final
Report. Although the functions of these buttons do not exactly
follow the sequence of activities for a PBL model of teaching,
collectively they do. The following is an alignment of the
functions of these buttons with the sequence of the PBL teaching
model:

- The Folder presents the intellectual confrontation.
- The Notebook presents understanding of the problem
- Books, Beaker, Monitor, and Graduation Cap, allow
  students to gather information. Learners list actions to be
  taken, which include Research Rack, Dr. D's Lab,
  questioning an expert, and other resources.

- The Notebook provides tools to analyze information and formulate a hypothesis based on the information that is gathered.
- The Character represents a tool for the students to provide a solution and prepare the final report.

One of the most effective features of the *NASA SCIence Files* is that all other episodes follow the same sequence of activities. Such consistency in design has proven to be an effective means of allowing students to benefit from an educational site rather than trying to figure out designs that vary.

Reflection

Before closing this chapter, it is essential to write a few words about the thematic interdisciplinary approach to the design of multimedia learning environments. The traditional approach to education and educational technology emphasizes isolation of disciplines. Although there are some benefits in a disciplinary approach to education, such as specialization, its disadvantages outweigh its advantages. There are several disadvantages in disciplinary education that need to be stated.

First, disciplinary education often ignores or downplays the holistic perspective. As mentioned at the beginning of this chapter, both nature and today's business community expect our graduates to think and solve problems from an interdisciplinary approach. Second, disciplinary education relies heavily on the teacher as the transmitter of information. There is a growing concern today that the goal of teachers is to become architects of educational settings in which students can understand the problems and be able to locate, gather, analyze information, and recommend solutions to them. Third, disciplinary education does not allow personal growth for the students. However, a thematic interdisciplinary education allows students to better serve themselves in their quest for personal growth and development of identity. Finally, a disciplinary education is not brain compatible; whereas, a thematic interdisciplinary education functions like students' brains do.

Part II
Orientation to Perceptual Design

Unlike the earlier days of computing when only a few highly skilled people were using computers, today the range of users and their knowledge about computers is huge. The evolutionary path that technology has taken in the last few decades to make it simple for just about anybody to use is mainly due to three landmarks that include Dynabook, the Star, and the Apple Lisa. Dynabook was the brainchild of Allan Kay who had a vision to design a responsive book-size personal computer with radio links to worldwide networks for personal needs. Alan Kay's concept influenced the development of the Star workstation by Xerox Park that used a mouse and simple interactivity between man and machine. Ultimately, the lessons learned from these two systems culminated in the development of Apple Lisa, a predecessor to today's Apple Macintosh.

The unifying theme beyond the success of these three computing systems is that they provided a form of simple and effective interface, known as Graphical User Interface (GUI), for the novice as well as expert. With the introduction of the Web by Tim Berners-Lee and HTML as a simple and effective authoring tool, both the highly skilled as well as novice became able to design and develop Web sites that only a few years ago were the realm of experts in computing.

The power and the flexibility of the Web allow educators to design and develop e-learning environments. Today, there are virtually an unlimited number of Web sites that have been authored by well-intentioned and intelligent educators. Not all of these Web sites are created equal. Some Web sites make everything look simple. When Web sites appear simple to the learner, even the most complex educational tasks become achievable for the students. On the other hand when Web sites are visually and cognitively confusing and cluttered, even the simplest tasks are impossible to carry out by the learner.

The success of the former educational Web site that makes everything look simple and elegant is mainly due to the ability of the designer to combine the visual and cognitive elements together in such a manner that the e-learning environments look simple, effective, and elegant to the learner. The knowledge to combine and present these visual and cognitive elements to design and develop simple and elegant educational Web sites lies within the field of interface design. The key to understanding the field of interface design is to focus on three different areas. These areas include foundations of interface design, visual design, and how learners interact with the e-learning environments to navigate through the content. To fully appreciate the contributions of the field of interface design to the design of e-learning environments, Part II includes the following four chapters.

Chapter Six is concerned with the foundations of interface design. This chapter opens up with a definition and the process of educational interface design. It continues with an overview of human perceptual theories and design techniques. Finally, the chapter concludes with some preliminary guidelines for interface design.

In Chapter Seven you will learn about visual interfaces. There will be detailed discussion and examples of design techniques and visual design elements such as icons, menus, typography, colors, and others. The reader will be introduced to the qualities of text, images, and colors, and the guiding principles of these building blocks of e-learning environments that allow for better presentation of interfaces.

Chapter Eight is further discussion of visual design elements such as animation, video, and audio. Chapter Eight also provides an introduction to Macromedia Flash MX, as the authoring tool of choice, whose features support incorporation of animation, sound, and video for e-learning.

Chapter Nine is concerned with page layout and site architecture for e-learning. Page layout focuses on how perceptual theories can assist in the proper arrangement of the basic elements of design on individual pages. Site architecture focuses on building the structures and organizational schemes that would satisfy the learners' educational needs.

While this part is an introduction to the field of interface design, I encourage you to further your knowledge about this highly promising field. At the end of the chapter I will provide a selected list of books, articles, and Web sites about interface design that are educationally related. These references will increase your knowledge about the field that will allow you to design and develop e-learning environments that are simple, effective, and elegant.

Chapter 6
Visual Design and E-learning

In the introduction to this book, I presented the concept that educational materials that are designed for e-learning environments can be viewed as the incoming information to be processed by the learner at two levels: perceptual and knowledge organization. Part I of this book is devoted to instructional design that is concerned with knowledge organization. In this part of the book, I shall delve into the topics related to perceptual design and visual interface organization.

The perceptual level is concerned with how educational materials are presented in terms of auditory, visual, interactivity, or the navigational modality. At this level the goal is to present educational materials such as text, audio, video, interactivities, and the organization of content in such a way to make the learners focus on what they need to perceive and learn. In order to achieve effective perceptual design, we have to have a basic understanding of perceptual theories and their ramifications to the visual design process. This chapter focuses on the following topics:

- Perceptual Design
- Psychology of Perception
    - Ecological Approach
    - Constructive Approach
    - Gestalt Laws of Perceptual Organization
- Language of Visual Communication
    - Elements of Design
    - Syntax of Design
        - Elegance and Simplicity
        - Scale, Contrast, and Proportion
        - Organization and Visual structure.
- Preliminary Guidelines

Perceptual Design

In our daily lives, we encounter numerous situations in that someone has designed something with which we interact. For example, while writing this book, I am sitting on a chair that somebody has thought about its design, or when you go to Disneyland the park has been designed based on the way people interact with it. How we interact with everyday things in our lives depends on our past experiences. If we encounter a situation that we do not understand how to interact with, we rely on our past perceptual experiences. Our perceptual knowledge of the world develops throughout our lives as the result of interaction with our surroundings. We carry our perceptual knowledge with us in our daily lives. Most of the time we interact naturally to our physical surroundings, other times we do not. The times that we do not interact naturally is when our perceptual knowledge does not match the new situation or physical objects that we have encountered. In these situations, we rely on our past perceptual knowledge to interact with the new situation or new object, which sometimes causes confusion.

In order to avoid confusion, designers must rely on the knowledge they have about human perception to design new objects so that they are compatible with human perception. This is especially true with the introduction of modern devices such as cars, computers, tape players, and the Web. The design of these new devices must be such that the users will not get confused or create embarrassing situations when they use them; for example, I recall a time when I parked my car while the engine was still running, and I locked the doors. Obviously, I called myself stupid for doing that, but was I? The solution is to design cars so that the doors cannot be locked with the key still inside the car.

Donald Norman in a popular book, *Design of Everyday Things* (1988), has described many modern and not so modern devices whose interfaces are confusing. For example, as Norman describes in his book, there have been instances where doors are designed in an unnatural way: "I push doors that are meant to be pulled, pull doors that should be pushed, and walk into doors that should be slid" (Norman, 1988, p. 3). In opening doors that are not designed with our past perceptual knowledge, we tend to cause embarrassing and sometimes dangerous situations. We generally blame ourselves in these situations. Norman, justifiably so, places the blame on the designers. He feels that an integral part of the design process is, "mental models, the models people have of themselves, others, the environment, and the things with which they interact. People form mental models through experience, training, and instruction" (Norman, 1988, p.17). As human beings we rely on our past perceptual experiences (mental models) in our everyday interactions with the world, including opening and closing doors. Norman's solution is to design new devices that are compatible with people's mental models or perceptual knowledge.

Unfortunately, the situation for e-learning design is much more critical in terms of creating Web sites that are compatible with the perceptual knowledge of the user. This is because the Web is a simple multimedia environment that allows anyone with a few hours of technical training to develop Web sites. Such development often occurs without any regard to the perceptual knowledge of the user. In fact, most Web sites are designed by people who ask questions like "When I am clicking on this button?" or "What color do I like?" or " Where would I like my logo?" Unfortunately, this is a typical mistake most novice designers make by assuming that they are designing for themselves. The first rule of effective Web design is to design for your users and not for yourself. Specially in the case of developing e-learning environments, developers and educators must go beyond their own likes and dislikes. The developers must see the Web site through the perceptual knowledge of their learners. They must have a basic knowledge of how students perceive things and how their perceptual knowledge is formed, and how their attentions can be focused on the perceptual design of the e-learning environments. In short, anyone who wishes to design e-learning environments must have an introduction to the psychology of perception.

Psychology of Perception

In order to interact with e-learning environments, students need to perceive the instructional materials that are presented through the interface in terms of their own perceptual knowledge. Designers and educators who are attempting to develop e-learning environments must have an understanding of how theories of perception can help in the design of the interface. There are two opposing and sometimes complimentary theories of perception. These two theories of visual perception are called ecological and constructive.

The Ecological Approach

The ecological approach describes perception as a direct process of detecting information from the objects in our surroundings (Gibson, 1979). The ecological approach is concerned with what we perceive in a continuous perceptual process. For example, in the ecological approach designers are concerned with the perception of an icon in a cluttered interface. They would like to find out the perceptual activities that are involved when a user detects an icon or an image.

The central concept of the ecological approach is the concept of affordance. Norman Donald explains the concept of affordance as "the term affordance refers to the perceived and actual properties of the thing, primarily those fundamental properties that determine just how the thing could possibly be used. A chair affords ("is for") support and, therefore, affords sitting" (Norman, 1988 p. 9). Therefore, affordance is the natural property of objects and permits specific perception of that object. For example, a flat white surface affords to be written on, or a button on a computer monitor affords to be clicked on. If we can find the natural properties of objects, then, we can design elements of interfaces that make their perception easier for the audience to use. In other words when affordance is natural and perceptually obvious, we interact with its design naturally.

Modern computers use the concept of affordance for the design of their Graphical User Interface (GUI). Figure 6.1 shows several examples of affordance (e.g. Windows, Close button) of modern interfaces. For example, it does not take any explanation that if you wish to delete a document, you can drag it to the Recycle Bin. The icon for the Recycle Bin on the desktop affords (is for) its function (deleting files). Or the Close button affords to be clicked on for the Window to be closed.

Figure 6.1 Affordance of Objects (Close Button)

The Constructive Approach

It is generally assumed by the novice that in order for our visual senses to perceive, we have templates of all objects in our memory. When we see a specific object in the environment, our brain matches that object with the appropriate template in our memory. This process, with the exception of matching images, is very similar to the way a camera captures images of our surroundings. The reality is that human visual perception and the human brain do not function like a camera.

Just imagine a simple letter A. There are an infinite number of ways such a letter can be presented in terms of its size, color, shape, orientation, etc. Considering the huge number of objects in our universe, it does not make sense for our brain to have evolved to memorize different templates for each object and their infinite variety. That would be a very complex and enormously complicated system. The human brain operates on simplicity, and a template-oriented approach to perception is not a simple process.

The constructive approach to perception posits that what we see is not a replica or copy of the objects in our surroundings. Instead, our visual perception operates on a simple process that is based on our prior knowledge of objects. We construct a model of that object in our surroundings by perceiving its distinctive features and putting them together through a set of organizational rules. Then we match the constructed image with our prior knowledge about the perceived object. For example, Figure 6.2 is a black and white image. At first glace the image looks like several series of black spots imposed on a white background. However, having the knowledge of what a dog looks like, we construct an image of a Dalmatian. This is an active construction of images by detecting the features and then combining these features according to some rules of perceptual organization.

Figure 6.2 Photograph of a Dalmatian (by R.C. James)

Figure 6.3 shows the same constructive approach for the letter E. In the construction of the letter E, we perceive the two distinctive features of horizontal and vertical lines. We put these features together through the principle of proximity and continuation (to be discussed below) to turn the three horizontal and one vertical line into the letter E. In the construction of the letter E, size, orientation, texture, and handwriting become irrelevant.

Figure 6.3 Constructive Approach to the Perception of Letter E

The constructive approach also emphasizes the importance of context in the process of perception. For example, Figure 6.4 illustrates how we perceive the same shape as different letters in different contexts. In the words the cat, the middle letter is exactly the same shape in both words. However, in the first word the middle shape is perceived as H, and in the second word the same shape is recognized as A. Although the middle letters in the two words are ambiguous, the context and our prior knowledge about the writing system enable us to correctly interpret the words the cat.

TAE CAT

Figure 6.4 The Effect of Context on Perception (Selfridge 1955)

The ecological and constructive theories give excellent explanations of visual perception. It is essential to note that these two theories are complementing each other rather than opposing. Both theories explain the active perceptual process of perception; however, while the constructive approach explains how our brain seeks patterns of features, the ecological theory describes perception of the whole. In other words while the subconscious mind looks for patterns in objects for constructing visual perception, the conscious mind finds the object from the clutter of other objects in the environment. A combination of these two theories explains more adequately the process of perception. For interface design purposes, one should design to teach consistent patterns to the subconscious mind, and arrange the elements of design for the conscious mind to detect.

The Gestalt Laws of Perceptual Organization

As mentioned above, the constructive approach explains perception in terms of the distinctive features of objects and a set of organizational rules. The question then is "What are the organizational rules?" The Gestalt psychologists of the 1920's were interested in discovering a set of perceptual laws that would allow grouping of the distinctive features of objects to be perceived. They believed that interpretations of the meaning of objects are based on humans having innate laws of perceptual organization. For example, Figure 6.5 illustrates that there are three circles and a triangle; however, in reality there are partial circles and no real triangle to be perceived. The Gestalt psychologists were interested in explaining the laws that would allow our visual perception to see the actual image as a triangle within three circles.

Figure 6.5 Perception of a Triangle within Three Circles

The Gestalt psychologists discovered that there are actually several laws of perceptual organization. Figure 6.6 shows the Gestalt laws: proximity, similarity, closure, continuity, area, and symmetry.

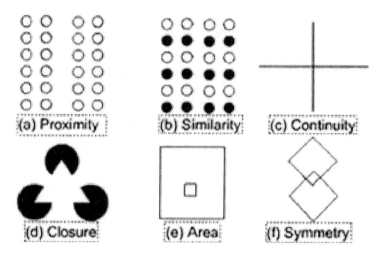

Figure 6.6 Gestalt Laws of Perceptual Organization

The principle of proximity explains why we group elements that are close to each other rather than see a random cluster of elements. Figure 6.6 (a) shows this concept at two levels. First, we group the circles into four vertical columns rather than individual circles. Second, because the first two columns and the last two columns are closer to each other, the whole figure is seen as two groups of two columns.

The principle of similarity explains why we group similar items of the same shape or color together as if they belong to each other. In Figure 6.6 (b), we perceive three rows of white circles and three rows of black circles as belonging to each other.

Continuity is the principle that explains perception of simple continuous contour rather than a complex and irregular shape. For example, Figure 6.6 (c) shows a simple perception of two lines traversing each other, rather than a more complex perception of four lines creating opposing angles.

Figures 6.6 (d) illustrates the principle of closure, which describe the human innate tendency of perceiving visual stimuli as a closed, complete shape instead of broken bits and pieces; therefore, the shapes in the figure appear to be composed of three circles and a triangle that superimposes itself on them. This example also relates to the principle of area as shown in Figure 6.6 (e). The principle of area states that a smaller figure is generally perceived as the foreground and the larger area as the background of an image. In both figures 6.6 (d) and (e), this is true where the larger circles and the rectangle are seen as background, and the triangle and the smaller rectangle are seen as foreground.

The last principle of the laws of perceptual organization is symmetry. This principle states that regions bounded by symmetrical borders are perceived as a whole rather the constituent parts that make up the whole. Therefore, figure 6.6 (f) shows that the figure is seen as two overlapping objects rather than three objects.

The principles of the Gestalt laws of perceptual organization have been used extensively in the interface design of successful software; for example, GUI designers group data together based on the principle of proximity. They color code elements of design based on the principle of similarity, and elements are placed in such a way to satisfy the principle of closure.

Language of Visual Communication

The main objective of perceptual design is to render a dynamic three-dimensional world into a static two dimensional computer screen so that it is appropriate to the users' perceptual knowledge. In traditional design such as painting, the designers were mostly concerned with rendering the aesthetic quality of the real world. In some rare cases traditional designers were concerned with the introduction of functionality; for example, in painting the Mona Lisa, Leonardo Da Vinci was probably concerned with the aesthetic quality of the painting as well as its function in terms of her smile.

In the design of modern interfaces, designers are obliged to communicate visually with the user in a way that is functional as well as aesthetically pleasing. More specifically, modern interfaces must be concerned with rendering more aspects of the real world into their design. They must be concerned with function, aesthetics, interactivity, three dimensionality, context, users' needs, and specific tasks that are present in the real world.

In order to accurately translate the qualities of the real world into the flat screen of a computer, there has to be a language of visual design by means of which the process of design can be implemented. Kevin Mullet and Darrell Sano (1995) in their groundbreaking book, *Designing Visual Interfaces: Communication Oriented Techniques,* have introduced the concept of a visual communication language:

> We refer frequently to visual language, by which we mean the visual characteristics (shape, size, position, orientation, color, texture, etc.) of a particular set of design elements (point, line, plane, volume, etc.) and the way they are related to one another (balance, rhythm, structure, proportion, etc.) in solving a particular communication problem. Any language system defines both a universe of possible signs and a set of rules for using them. Every visual language thus has a formal vocabulary containing the basic design elements from which higher-level representations are assembled, and a visual syntax describing how elements may be combined within that system.

Elements of Design

In this book, I shall follow the tradition established by Mullet and Sano (1995). The elements of design (formal vocabulary) of any e-learning environment should include discussion of icons, imagery, text, color, audio, video, dialog boxes, and navigational systems. Chapter Seven, Eight and Nine are devoted to detailed discussion of the basic elements of design. In the remainder of this chapter I will describe the visual syntax describing how elements may be combined to create interfaces that are pleasing to the eye as well as simple to use.

Syntax of Design

In what follows, I shall concentrate on discussion of the design techniques that Mullet and Sano (1995) call the syntax of design. I shall limit my discussion of these techniques to three categories; (1) *elegance and simplicity, (2) scale, contrast, proportion, and (3) organization and visual structure.* These techniques can later be applied to combine the basic elements of design together so that the outcome of design is compatible with the perceptual knowledge of the learner/user.

Elegance and Simplicity

Simplicity does not mean dull or boring. According to Mullet and Sano (1995) simplicity is the most important element of design. The best place to look for simplicity and elegance in design is in nature. A rose, for example, is a simple and elegant design, yet it has a very complex structure that has been made transparent through the design that nature has provided for it.

To achieve simplicity in design, one must either be a genius or one must learn certain principles and techniques. Not all of us are geniuses in design. However, there are some principles that have been followed by many not so genius artists over the years that allow the creation of simple and elegant design. These principles are *unity, refinement, and fitness.*

Unity is achieved when two or more elements of design are combined to produce a coherent whole. A great example of how unity is used to create a logo is seen in Figure 6.7. The Tennis Master Series logo captures its audience by unifying tennis strokes. The two elliptical paths represent the forehand and the backhand strokes, which produces a simple but meaningful design to its audience.

Figure 6.7 Unity of Design

Unity is not restricted to logos. Web sites that tie the various basic elements of page design together appear to be simple and elegant. A unified page design is first seen as a whole. Unity can be achieved by using some of the Gestalt laws of organization; for example, merging one element into another uses the concept of closure, or grouping elements of design uses the principle of proximity.

Refinement is a method of achieving simplicity and elegance by continuously eliminating the elements of design that are not necessary. The process starts with the initial design. The designer must examine every element of the design and identify those elements that are not needed to communicate the goal. For example, Figure 6.8 shows the process of unity and refinement in which I designed a logo for parenting for a Web site. The goal was to unify two elements (a mother and a child) to show parenting, and then refine it to its minimum size for the Web. The design started with the figure on the left, and after a series of refinements the final design was rendered as the figure on the right.

Figure 6.8 Unity and Refinement

Fitness is achieved when design fits purpose; in other words, the design affords the purpose of the design. In modern GUI design, the majority of menu systems that have been developed fit the purpose. For example, Figure 6.9 shows the design of tools for *Macromedia Flash*, which is an animation tool for the Web. As seen in the figure, the design fits the purpose and there is no need for explanation of what each tool can do.

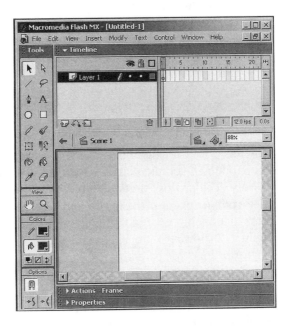

Figure 6.9 Tools in Flash

In addition to the principles of simplicity and elegance such as unity, refinement, and fitness, there are some techniques that one can use to achieve simplicity and elegance in design. These techniques are *reduction, regularization, and leverage.* Mullet and Sano (1995) have the following recommendations for the techniques they use to achieve simplicity and elegance:

Reduction:
- Determine the essential qualities
- Critically examine each element and decide why you need it
- Remove the element(s). If it is still functional and aesthetically pleasing, then the elements are not needed

Regularization:
- Use regular form, color, size, graphics
- Limit variation
- Critical elements should not be regularized

Leverage:
- Review each element and their function
- Question if two or more elements can be combined
- Combine into one element

Scale, Contrast, and Proportion

When an interface is visually offensive it is often because the designer does not have a good understanding of the principles of scale, contrast, and proportion. According to Mullet and Sano (1995, p.51), " The subtle interrelationship of scale, contrast, and proportion can be seen in every harmonious design." As the first step towards creating a balanced relationship between elements of design, I shall first define scale, contrast, and proportion. Then I will discuss the techniques to achieve a balanced interrelationship of scale, contrast, and proportion.

Scale refers to the relationship that exists between the relative sizes of the elements of design. Figure 6.10 shows the ability of designers to use scale. In this interface from *Microsoft Dinosaurs*, the designer wanted to show the size of the dinosaurs, and he is showing it by comparing their sizes with the height of people and the building in the background.

Figure 6.10 Scale Is Essential to Show the Magnitude

Proportion in design deals with the ratio, rather than size, between the elements of design. The best example of how proportion can be used is seen in the classical Golden Rectangle. A golden rectangle is appealing to the eye because of the ratio between its length and its width, which is 1 to 1.6, respectively. The proportional size in many instances of design determines the underlying structure of a design.

Contrast can be seen in the differences among the elements of design. Contrast can result from differences in shape, size, color, position, texture, and orientation. For example, Figure 6.11 shows how the Microsoft CD-ROM for *Ancient Lands* uses contrast between a hand-drawn image, photograph, and sculpture to reveal the message of the diversity in the drama and theater of Ancient Greece.

Figure 6.11 Use of Contrast

There are some techniques that one can use to achieve harmony for scale, contrast, and proportion. These techniques are *layering and integrating*.

Layering is a technique for creating distinct regions for an interface. Layering can happen with scale, contrast, and proportion. For example, contrast in color, shape, or orientation can create a layering effect for grouping elements of design. Integration is the technique of creating a unified impression of one or two elements of design. Generally integration is the infusion of the background image into the foreground figure. Integration requires that the scale of the background and the foreground be carefully matched. Figure 6.12 shows how the interface design for the Web site is using layering to create distinct regions, contrast of color to separate the regions, and integration of the background into the whole interface.

Figure 6.12 The Use of Layering and Integration

Organization and Visual Structure

Effective arrangement of the elements of the interface as well as effective organization of content is the key for successful e-learning environments. When the organizational design is not in control of the learner's visual preference, then the whole purpose of communicating with the learner fails. The key to successful design of e-learning environments is to organize both the interface as well as the content to satisfy the needs of the learner.

The principles that guide effective organization are *grouping, hierarchy, relationship, and balance*. The process of organization begins with grouping the elements together. Grouping allows learners to deal with the intricacies of design through the Gestalt laws of organization such as proximity, similarity, and continuity. As mentioned before, effective grouping maybe also be done by shape, color, orientation, function, texture, dialog boxes, etc.

Once grouping is achieved, the proper hierarchy of groups should be established. Such a hierarchy not only will decide on the navigational system, but also is the key to proper organization of the content. Next, organizational design must create a logical relationship among the elements and the groups in the hierarchy. Relationships between the elements are best achieved by the dominance of size and position because the eye is very sensitive to alignment of position and size. Finally, the organization and the visual structure of the e-learning environments must be balanced in terms of interface composition. Balance of the interface can be achieved by symmetry, asymmetry, color, shape, and alignment. Figure 6.13 shows how the design of the Macintosh operating system has achieved grouping, hierarchy, and relationship in the design of the dialog box for opening documents.

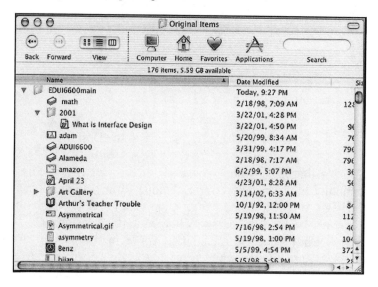

Figure 6.13 Grouping, Hierarchy, and Relationship

The most effective techniques to achieve appropriate organization and visual structure are symmetry, alignment, and the use of white space. Symmetry provides a great method for organizing the elements of an interface. Figure 6.14 shows how the Chinese yin-yang symbol has implemented the technique of symmetry to evoke the idea of duality. In modern interfaces sometimes asymmetry is used as another technique to achieve organization and effective visual structure. Interface designers juxtapose heavy elements of design with lighter ones to achieve effective asymmetry in their design.

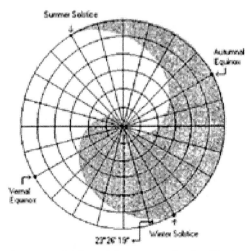

Figure 6.14 Use of Symmetry in the Design

Alignment, which is based on the Gestalt concept of continuity, is a very effective technique for arranging elements of design to reduce complexity. Alignment is the key technique for greater balance and harmony in the interface design.

White space is the unused space in the design of an interface. In reality the white space acts as the background to the interface design. In recent years there has been a tendency by designers to use every available pixel on the interface. This is generally seen on the majority of Web sites for newspapers. This may prove to be detrimental to design. Too much information creates a cluttered design, and the process to read everything on a monitor to find what they want is too taxing on the users. On the other hand, the use of too much white space is not an effective technique for design. It is really essential to understand that white space is needed to attract the learner, and guide their visual path to the elements that the design has in mind. Designers must balance their use of white space to guide the viewer's eyes to the elements on the screen.

Reflection:

Before closing this chapter, the golden rule of interface design is to place the needs of the user (learner) at the heart of the design process. Since user centered design is based on the perception of the user, it is essential to pay attention to some preliminary guidelines that would satisfy the perceptual needs of the student. IBM, a leader in the field of interface design has placed a great deal of effort to carry out research and development in this field. Their Ease of Use group is a giant in the field of interface design. Their web site http://www-3.ibm.com/ibm/easy has provided valuable design guidelines for experts. They recommend the following basic design guidelines as the principles that form the foundation of good design. For detailed discussion of the following preliminary guidelines, please visit the Ease of Use Website.

- Simplicity: Don't compromise usability for function

- Support: Place the user in control and provide proactive assistance

- Familiarity: Build on users' prior knowledge

- Obviousness: Make objects and their controls visible and intuitive

- Encouragement: Make actions predictable and reversible

- Satisfaction: Create a feeling of progress and achievement

- Availability: Make all objects available at all times

- Safety: Keep the user out of trouble

- Versatility: Support alternate interaction techniques

- Personalization: Allow users to customize

- Affinity: Bring objects to life through good visual design

Chapter 7
Text, Color, Images, and Icons

Although audio, video, and fancy animation have come to be the playground for multimedia designers in recent years, text, images, and color are still the most effective and widely used multimedia components for the design of e-learning environments. Text has a universal appeal, and it can enhance a Web site to attract a great number of people. Text has the added value of linking it to other media in most creative ways. Because of such a wide appeal, text can be used for multimedia content, menus, buttons, and navigational systems. Attractive images and illustrations also appeal to people's perception of any Web site. Graphics often enhance Web sites and add an aesthetic beauty to the site that no other media can do. The use of appropriate colors allows the personalizing of e-learning environments. A basic understanding of the nature of color and how it can be used to enhance e-learning is essential. The purpose of this chapter is to introduce the reader to the qualities of text, images, and colors, and to discuss the guiding principles of these building blocks of e-learning environments that allow for better presentation of interfaces. To achieve these goals, I shall discuss the following topics in this chapter:

- Working with Text
  - Text and Its Origin in Technology
  - Serif and Sans Serif
  - The Use of Text in E-learning Environments
  - Design Guidelines for Text
- Working with Color
  - Color Theories
  - Psychological Effect
  - Design Guidelines for Colors
- Working with Images
  - Bitmapped or Vector-Based Images
  - Ways of Dealing with Images
    - Clip Art
    - Scanned Images
    - Tracing Images

Working with Text

In modern times, hardly a day goes by that we do not use text to convey information. With the introduction of the Web as a means to convey e-learning information, the role of text has become even more vital. In e-learning development, text assumes three major functions: the titles (what it is about), the content (educational materials to be presented), and the navigational system (interactivity and the menu). In this section, a brief look at the origin of text in multimedia and the Web is presented, followed by a description of its function. Some useful design guidelines for text are presented that research has shown to be effective in the development of e-learning.

Text and Its Origin in Technology

Text was originally created on computers by programs written for applications such as word processing. The ability to change text on computers was limited to upper and lower case letters. Boldface and underlined styles were later added as one of the functions of word processors. With the introduction of Macintosh and other personal computers, bitmapping was used to create text.

In a bitmapped approach, text characters are actually small graphic files. Characters are created by arrangement of pixels (stands for picture elements, which are individual points on the screen). The computer stores various fonts, sizes and styles of different characters or letters. Figure 7.1 shows an enlarged bitmap of the texts in my daughter's name (Roya), where each square represents one pixel on the screen.

Figure 7.1 Bitmap Representations of Letters

The early personal computers (e.g. Macintosh) used 72 pixels per inch (ppi) to display bitmapped text and graphics on the screen. The major problems with bitmap-based texts were the amount of memory required for storing all possible fonts with their various sizes and styles, and the low resolution of the printed materials. To improve upon the storage, speed, and resolution problems for characters in different sizes, a small company called Adobe developed the *PostScript language*.

Adobe is no longer a small company, thanks to PostScript and other innovations developed within this creative establishment. PostScript uses mathematical formulas, not bitmapping, to create fonts. Because it relies on mathematical construction, characters can be resized, reshaped, and restyled without loosing their appearance. Furthermore, characters can be processed much faster than bitmapped fonts because of the mathematical construction of the PostScript language. The main problem with the original version of the PostScript language was that it was designed for printed materials. On the screen, characters were still being represented by the bitmap procedure. To eliminate this problem, Adobe developed *Adobe Type Manager (ATM)*. This product allowed multimedia developers to display virtually any size and style of font on the screen. Furthermore, because ATM also functions on the bases of mathematical formulas, manipulation of color and special effects for text were made much easier on the screen.

At the same time that ATM was being offered by Adobe, Apple also introduced its own version of formula-based fonts called *True Type*. It was designed to replace bitmapped fonts and to compete with Adobe. TrueType provided the printing of smooth characters on a printer and displayed better looking text on the monitor. Today, Windows' and Mac's operating systems support True Type, PostScript, and ATM.

Since bitmapped text has a staircase effect, one way to soften the edges of the text is by adding transitional colors (or different shades of the same color) to smooth the jagged edges of the text. This process has come to be known as anti-aliasing. Figure 7.2 shows the effect of anti-aliasing on the appearance of text. Both lines of text were created using *Photoshop* with the same font, size and style. However, in the upper line, anti-aliasing was selected in Photoshop.

Roya
Roya

Figure 7.2 Anti-Aliasing Smoothes the Edges

Serif and Sans serif

Today Web developers have a variety of options in fonts, size, and styles. However, though many fonts exist, they all generally fall into two categories for e-learning production: serif and sans serif (Figure 7.3). Serifs are the small flags or decorations that end a letter stroke. The best examples of serif fonts are Times, Palatino, and New Century. Sans serif is French for without decoration. Examples of sans serif fonts include Helvetica, New York, Chicago, and Arial.

Times   Arial

Figure 7.3 Serif and Sans Serif

Fonts can either be acquired or created. Today, the market is saturated with a variety of fonts for e-learning developers. The choice for the designer includes a variety of Serif and sans serif fonts in bitmap, PostScript, and True Type.

In using these fonts, it is essential to remember that not all end users have access to all different fonts. One approach to solving the problem of fonts access is for the developer to include the fonts used in a separate folder within production. However, this may violate copyright protection laws. Obviously, the best approach is not to take a chance and license the right to use.

One of the most critical aspects of using fonts for e-learning environments is the size of text you choose. Obviously the most appropriate size of font depends on the context of use and the audience. Choose fonts, style, and size that are the most effective for your particular e-learning environment. Always test your choice of fonts with your audience.

The Use of Text in E-Learning Environments

As mentioned previously, the functions of text in development of e-learning environments are for titles, content and navigation.

Titles and headings tell the user what the e-learning is all about. The use of different font styles for the title, the content, and the menu is to be avoided because it confuses the reader. Generally, titles are displayed with the same font as the content except the former appears in sans serif and in a larger font size. To make titles more professional looking, appealing, and legible, both upper and lower case are to be used. The title should use anti-aliasied text to give it a professional look.

Content in e-learning is referred to as the educational information one wishes to convey to the students. Content in e-learning is not limited to text; in addition, it can be graphics, video, or animation. In most cases, content in e-learning is conveyed by the integration of one or more media in the production. In using pre-existing content, multimedia producers must be careful about obtaining the right to use such content.

One of the most appealing characteristics of text in e-learning is its potential as a navigational tool. Navigational systems include both the menu as well as other interactivities. Any text can become a button or an anchor that the user clicks on to navigate to the intended content or other specified URL. The ability to link text to content is referred to as hypertext.

Hypertext was initially coined by Ted Nelson to describe linking of text in a non-linear fashion. The word hyper actually denotes linking. In e-learning, a text or group of texts can be linked to any other text or group of texts. The success of the World Wide Web and browsers like Explorer and Netscape is heavily dependent upon the function of hypertext.

The ability to link through text can be either internal or external. Internal links are saved in the server where the e-learning site resides. External links are information residing on other servers. In either case, interactivities can take the form of navigational systems such as a menu or links to elaborate on the topics. Figure 7.4 shows how links can serve as a sidebar menu system. Here the menu items to the left serve as a navigational system. As each menu item is selected, new information appears on the main content area. The menu items can appear on the top, the left, or in other positions.

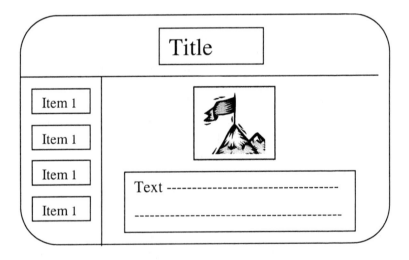

Figure 7.4 Text as Menu, Title, and Content

Basic Design Guidelines for Text

Text in e-learning must be presented effectively to convey information. The following are some basic design guidelines for effective display of text in multimedia presentations.

- Provide enough space for text to be visually appealing and legible.
- Use a serif font for the title and a sans serif font for display.
- Use both upper and lower case letters. (All uppercase letters are difficult to read on the monitor.)
- Avoid using red on black for the body because it is very difficult to read.
- Black text on a white background or black text on a yellow background is the easiest to read on the monitor.
- Avoid decorative fonts for the body of the text.
- Vary the font size for the title, navigational system, and the content.
- Use anti-aliasing for the title.
- Limit the amount of text on computer monitors for content. Too much text on the screen is not appealing to users/learners.
- Choose the font, style, and size that are more effective for a particular production.

Working with Colors

To develop text, images, animation, or video for e-learning environments, Web designers ask the following questions regarding the use of colors:

- Which color should I use?
- How many colors should I use?
- Are these colors appropriate?
- How can I improve the colors I have used to please my audience?

To be able to answer some of the previous questions, it is helpful to first briefly discuss how light and color work. Such knowledge provides the basis for better understanding of colors, and their effect on images, animation, or video in e-learning development.

Human eyes have two types of receptors to perceive colors. These receptors are called rods and cones. Rods are responsible to register light and dark, or the relative brightness of objects. Cones perceive colors. There are three kinds of cones. Each one responds to red light, green light, and blue light. Red, green, and blue are the primary colors. These same colors have been used to design computer monitors. Therefore the discussion below about the nature of light also applies to the composition of colors for computer monitors.

The source of any light (such as the sun or computer monitor) emits uniform light waves in all directions. Light waves have different wavelengths that determine the colors we perceive. For example, the color red is the result of the longest light wave, and the shortest light wave causes the color violet. The other colors (green, yellow, blue, and indigo) that we see in a rainbow are in between the red and the violet light waves.

In real life humans do not perceive individual and distinct colors. In fact, the millions of colors that are present in nature result from different light wavelengths blending into each other. Human visual color perception is the result of two types of light -- direct and reflected.

Direct light is perceived directly from the source such as the sun, a light bulb or computer monitor. Our perception of color from a direct light source is based on the trichromatic theory of color. The trichromatic theory posits that there are three primary colors: red, green, and blue. Combinations of these primary colors in varying degrees create different colors. Full mixture of these primary colors creates white, and absence of the three primary colors results in black or lack of color. Absence of one of the primary colors while the other two primary colors are blended creates a complementary color. For example, red and green yield yellow. Perception of color from direct light, therefore, is additive in nature because as different degrees of primary colors are added, new colors are created. Figure 7.5 shows how various colors result from blending or adding various mixtures of the three primary colors.

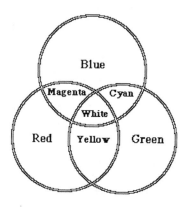

Figure 7.5 Additive Primary Colors (Burger, 1994)

Table 7.1 shows the RGB (Red, Green, and Blue) model that some graphic programs (e.g. Photoshop) use to create colors. These software functions on the additive theory of colors. A number ranging between 0 and 256 sets the amount of red, green, and blue. The numbers in the table illustrate that when the value of the three primary colors is zero, the result is black. On the opposite scale, when the full values of these three primary colors are combined the color that is perceived is white.

Table 7.1 The RGB Model (Burger, 1994)

Red	Green	Blue	Color
256	256	256	White
256	256	0	Yellow
256	o	256	Magenta
0	256	256	Cyan
256	0	0	Red
0	256	0	Green
0	0	256	Blue
0	0	0	Black

Humans generally do not look directly at a source of light. In fact, a majority of colors that humans perceive is the result of the reflective nature of wavelengths. That is, objects in nature do not have any color. However, different objects absorb and reflect different wavelengths from the same light source. The wave length(s) that is reflected from an object determines the color we perceive. For example, a red apple absorbs all wavelengths except the long wavelength of light that results in human perception as the color red. Then when one says grass is green, it simply means that the chemical chlorophyll in grass absorbs all wavelengths except the one for the color green that is reflected back into the atmosphere. It is interesting to note that when grass dies during winter, it no longer produces chlorophyll; therefore, some other chemical balance determines which wavelengths are absorbed and which ones are reflected.

Just as there are primary colors for human perception of direct light, there are three primary colors for reflected light. These primary colors for reflected light are cyan, magenta, and yellow. The chemical balance of each object in nature determines the degree of each of these primary reflected colors. Figure 7.6 shows that the colors humans perceive are the result of a subtractive mixture of cyan, magenta, and yellow.

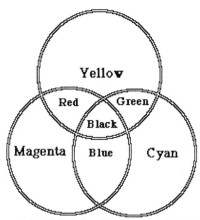

Figure 7.6 Subtractive Model of Reflected Light (Burger, 1994)

While principles of the subtractive color theory are directly applied to printed material, it is the additive theory for direct light that is more relevant to multimedia. In multimedia production one is more concerned with the images on the monitor as the direct source of light perception rather than the printed version of the production.

Most monitors are cathode-ray-tubes that function on the principles of the additive color theory. The way a monitor functions is very similar to the way impressionist painters create a painting. Instead of mixing paint on the palette, impressionist painters applied pure color in individual spots thus creating impressions of different colors in an image. Similarly the inside part of the face of a computer monitor is covered with thousands of phosphorous dots. These dots are actually a collection of three smaller chemically treated primary colors of red, green, and blue phosphorous dots. Each tightly grouped collection of dots of the three primary colors appears as a single dot on the monitor to the human eye. This is very similar to the way impressionist painters present images on canvas.

Computer monitors are also equipped with electron guns in the back. When voltage is applied to these electron guns, a specific color is triggered on the face of the monitor. Various voltage intensities and the pattern of the electrical currents determine the shape and the colors of images on the computer monitors. In other words, the degree of voltage determines the proportion of the primary colors that are added to create specific color on the monitor.

Psychological Effect

In addition to research and theories on colors, scientists have conducted experiments on how the human brain processes colors when they are perceived through the eyes. Two areas of research that are directly related to colors and technology are emotion and cultural association.

Because of human evolution and the effect of culture, colors have certain associations with our emotions. For example, because the color of the sky is blue, our brain usually relates that color with comfort and calmness. Table 7.2 provides a useful emotional association for different colors. You should analyze your audience and carefully select the color you wish to use to communicate a certain mood or emotion to your audience.

Table 7.2 Colors Associations (Adopted from Burger, 1994)

Color Association		
Color	**Perception**	**Examples**
Red	Alert, danger, sexy, hot	Stop sign, hell, roses, blood
Orange	Attention	Sun
Blue	Confident, royal, comfort	Sky, water, ribbon
Yellow	Loyalty, fun	Yellow rose
Green	Nature, clean, doing	Forest, money, go
Brown	Earth	Dirt, national parks
White	Purity, cleanliness	Clouds, heaven
Black	Elegant, mysterious	Night, death
Saturated	Loud, bold, capable	Logos, flags

In general cool colors such as blue and purple seem to recede into the distance; therefore, they are good choices for background colors. Warm colors, such as red, yellow, or orange appear to advance toward the audience; therefore, they are great colors for images in the foreground. These effects are also due to the ways the red, green, and blue cones are distributed in the eye.

Colors also have cultural associations. For example, in Western culture yellow means caution, red means danger, and purple means regal. There are also cultural differences. While in Western culture black symbolizes mourning, in Japanese culture white symbolizes the same concept. Colors can also represent corporations. For example, the color yellow is associated with Kodak. In using colors to communicate certain emotions, you should carefully analyze your audience so that your choice will not offend anyone.

Design Guideline for Colors

- Use a maximum of five plus or minus two colors. For novice users, four distinct colors are appropriate. This is because of the limitations of short-term memory (20 seconds). If you have to use more than three colors, then use spectral order in coding colors (ROY G BIV). Research has shown that viewers see spectral order as natural. For example, Red, Green, and Blue are generally viewed as Front, Middle, and Back respectively.
- Use central and peripheral colors appropriately. This is because there are more red and green cones in the center. There are more blue cones in the periphery. Blue is good for background or large areas. It is not good for lines, text or small shapes. In most cases black and white for backgrounds works just like blue. Red and green are good for a central position to capture attention.
- Use the same color for grouping. Always be consistent with color grouping.
- Use high chroma colors to attract attention, to signal danger, to remind your audience of a specific task, to attract older viewers, or for long viewing periods.
- Use colors to enhance black and white information.
- Use color in proper context with other colors.
- General guidelines for colors include the following:

  - To direct attention
  - To speed search
  - To aid recognition
  - To show organization
  - To rate or to quantify
  - To attract users
  - To reinforce emotion

Working with Images

Images convey a silent and potentially powerful message to users of educational multimedia. Educators have always been aware of the power and the function of images for conveying educational content to their students. However, image presentation for e-learning has been difficult because of file size. As in text, images also fall into two different categories. These two categories are bitmapped and vector-based object-oriented.

Bitmapped or Vector-Based Images

Bitmapped images are created by programs that change the color of individual pixels. Computer monitors are pixel based. That is, horizontally and vertically, they represent a number of dots as rows and columns. When these rows and columns intersect, they create so many pixels. For example, the standard color screen size has 640 horizontal and 480 vertical pixels. The result is a resolution of 640x480 pixels. When each pixel's color is changed, for example from white to black, then images can be created. In bitmapped drawing, resizing and reshaping is not supported. To resize or reshape an image, one must erase the original and redraw accordingly. As a general rule bitmapped images have larger file size than vector-based images.

Object-oriented or vector-based graphics are created by drawing lines, boxes, circles and other geometric shapes. In current literature, vector graphics refer to the same principle as object oriented graphics. That is, vector drawing is based on the line between two points: a starting point and an ending point. A mathematical formula or programming code determines the function of the line to create geometric shapes. Combinations of one or more of these geometric shapes are used to create images. Because these geometric shapes are mathematically expressed in angles, coordinates, and distance, they can be manipulated, resized, and moved after they are drawn, and they occupy much less storage on computers than bitmapped graphics.

These images are not a collection of pixels, but are each mathematical description of where the shape exists on the page and where its origin and end points are. In other words, a rectangle is saved as a coded description of the object. A rectangle may have the following code as its definition: RECT 10,10,30,20. These numbers are converted on an x and y axis as lines where the first line may start at x=10, y=10 point of the screen, then the line continues 30 pixels horizontally then 20 vertically. This creates a rectangle on the monitor. Furthermore the code: RECT 10,10,30,20, BLUE, GREEN creates the same rectangle with a blue border and green fill inside the shape. When graphics are created by object-oriented software such as *Adobe Illustrator or Macromedia Freehand*, they become easy to move, delete, resize, change color, or distort. Other graphic programs, like Photoshop, provide an extremely sophisticated environment for manipulating bitmapped graphics.

These two types of graphic categories, bitmapped and object-oriented, come in different formats. One of the problems of working with images in a multimedia production, especially if they are to be distributed on a network or on the Internet, is the transfer time. Both bitmapped and object-oriented images require large size files. These files need to be reduced in size or compressed. Fortunately, the majority of sophisticated programs provide the means to convert one format into another. The following is a brief description of some of these formats used by Macintosh and Windows programs:

- PICT (for PICTure) was originally designed to move graphics between programs on Macintosh. This format supports both bitmapped and object-oriented graphics.
- TIFF (for Tagged Image File Format) was originally designed by Aldus for the purpose of scanning images into computers. The most common popular programs that use TIFF are Photoshop and ColorStudio. Although TIFF is widely used on both Macintosh and Windows platforms today, its major disadvantage is that files cannot be compressed. Thus, they occupy a large amount of storage space and they are not suitable for e-learning.
- EPS is one of the most widely used graphic formats on a Windows platform. It supports both bitmapped as well as object-oriented graphics. EPS (Encapsulated PostScript) files are generally large

and include low resolution. Because of the low quality resolution of EPS files, they are not suitable for multimedia presentation on screen.

- GIF (Graphics Interchange Format) was designed by CompuServe to minimize transfer time when loading or unloading images. It has become popular among developers as a reliable source of clip art and scanned images for the Web. GIF is excellent for blocks of colors in images that do not exceed 256 colors. This means that images such as photographs that use shades of colors that exceed 256 colors are not suitable to be in GIF format.

- JPEG (Joint Photographic Experts Group) is suitable for e-learning environments for images that have lots of colors and shades of colors. What is good about JPEG is that its compression methods approximate colors that are available in the palette. This process saves more disk space and in some instances the file size is even less than GIF.

Images require large amounts of storage in a multimedia production. The size of the image file may not affect the multimedia title on a CD-ROM; however, placing an image on the Internet may adversely affect the e-learning environment production. One of the most significant features of different image formats is compression that reduces file size, thus making it easier to send over the Internet.

Currently GIF is the format of choice of images on the Net. GIF uses a lossless algorithm. This process allows compression of the original image and restructuring of the original values of an image upon loading. Other image formats such a JPEG use lossy algorithms in which less essential features for human perception are eliminated during compression. Although JPEG may be a valuable format, it does not restructure all the original values upon decompression, thus it loses some quality.

Ways of Dealing with Images

Thus far, graphics and images have been discussed as being created or edited on different applications from scratch. Programs such as Illustrator, Photoshop, and Freehand are great for creating or editing images. The other popular approaches to capturing images are clip art, scanning, and tracing. You will still need the above programs for editing these images

Clip Art

Some Web developers find it easier and less time-consuming to import or copy images from other sources, rather than making them from scratch. For this reason many companies have created clip art for a variety of purposes such as education or business. These clip art graphics are shipped on floppy disks or CD-ROM and they contain images, photographs, and even sound and video. Some programs also include clip art as part of the software; for example, Flash and Director from Macromedia. One of the most useful clip arts that can be used by *PowerPoint* and *Word from Microsoft* is *Microsoft Publisher*. It is offered on CD-ROM or online. The CD-ROM version of this product is an excellent resource. However, the online version (Design Gallery Live Website) can be found at: (http://dgl.microsoft.com/?CAG=1).

There are other publishing companies. Below you will find the URLs to some of these sites:

- Reallybig.com
  (http://reallybig.com/mcat.php3?mid=9)
- Kitty's Page Works
  (http://www.snowcrest.net/kitty/hpages/index.ht
  ml)
- ClipArt.com (http://www.free-graphics.com/)
- ArtToday (http://www.clipart.com/index.html)

Scanned Images

For educators who are not happy with clip art or who cannot find images that fit their need, scanning images is the next logical step. Flatbed scanners and handheld scanners are relatively cheap and of excellent quality. It is interesting that some of the better scanners are shipped with Photoshop. Considering the price of Photoshop and its excellent editing quality, flatbed scanners that are shipped with Photoshop are indeed a bargain

Amazingly, Web developers have become so obsessed with computers that many have abandoned the traditional approach to images. E-learning developers should be reminded that pencil, paper, and other means of drawing still have a place in multimedia. Images can first be developed on paper, and then digitized with high quality scanners.

Trace Images

Another, though less popular approach to digitizing images is to capture them by tracing pictures with a digitized pen or a mouse on a tablet. You can place an image on the tablet and trace the image with a pen or a mouse. The tracing of images by the pen or the mouse is captured by programs such as Illustrator or Flash. Companies such as WACOM (http://www.wacom.com/productinfo/index.cfm) offer digitized pen and tablets for tracing images onto your computer. The product form *WACOM* works with most graphics software such as Flash, or Illustrator. Fortunately, these products are relatively inexpensive. They are also a fun and practical approach to creating your own images.

For those educators who have the time and devotion, the best and most economical approach is to use graphic programs to create their own images. Scanned images are the next most economical alternative for capturing images.   With the availability of clip art for virtually any topic, they have become another viable choice for e-learning projects.

Basic Design Guideline for Images

- Analyze both students and the content, and then decide on the colors for images.

- Combine colors attractively to appeal to students. (For example, the color orange attracts attention while the color blue creates a non-threatening environment.)
- Avoid flat images. Use of distinct foreground elements in an image provides depth.
- Do not confine images in rectangular frames.
- Create implied motion by providing angles in an image.
- Remember images should convey information rather than be an art piece.
- Keep image placement consistent to avoid confusion.
- Scale both images and text appropriately.

Working with Icons

Icons are small images that have become very popular in all kinds of Web sites. One of the main reasons for their popularity is that they are extremely useful. They can be used to activate menus, perform actions, select tools, toggle between modes, manipulate windows, to point to other objects, represent files, or represent other items. Icons are also great for e-learning because they help learners to work smarter because conceptually icons are easier to recognize than text.

Types of Icons

There are a great variety of icons that have been designed for different Web sites. They can be categorized as

- Similie: direct comparison
- Metaphor: abstract symbols representing the concept
- Conceit: create a new way of representing the concept

Similie

Similies are icons that are directly representing a physical or emotional state. For example, Figure 7.7 shows how an image of books can directly represent books.

Figure 7.7 Books as an Icon

Metaphor

Metaphoric icons are abstract symbols representing a concept. Such comparison is generally indirect, and there may have to be some education for the user to recognize the concept. For example, a flashlight representing search on the Web may at first glance not to be recognized. A little education is sometimes necessary for the users to get to know the concept. Metaphoric icons have been over used in the design of Web sites. They do provide a momentary boost the first time, but sometimes are not very effective long term. Metaphoric icons come in a variety of ways such as textual, shape, analogy and motion. For example, a pencil may represent creativity, a chain may represent hyperlink, a question mark may represent help, or a broken arrow may represent peace.

Conceit

Conceits are icons that are newly created, and they are easily learned. Sometimes conceits are difficult to understand. For example, a majority of GUI interface icons such as windows, mouse, menu, or toolbars, were newly created by the designers. However, after some education through repeated usage, they became permanently etched into the users memory. This is like brand names (MacDonald, Tylenol, Bayer); symbols are created, then they are imbued with meaning. Figure 7.8 shows several icons that were newly created to represent atomic radiation, poison, mouse, and movies. The icons did not initially mean very much to people. However, after repeated exposure to them, they were etched into people's memories, and they need no explanation.

Figure 7.8 Icons that Were Newly Created

Design Guideline for Icons

- Keep them simple
- Keep them clear
- Keep them consistent
- Keep them familiar
- Design the initial icons by creating quick sketches
- Use color with discretion
- Evaluate by showing to potential users

Reflection

Before closing this chapter, it is essential to note that there are specific steps that one needs to take in the process of text, color, image, and icon design. Most designers, as the first step, sit in front of a computer and open a graphics application. In many instances they go through numerous designs for days and waste their time. It is really important to use pencil and paper and to follow a design procedure. In the following I will provide some steps that are necessary in the process of icon design; however, the same steps could be applied to creating images, text, or choosing colors for your audience:

1. Analyze the users by using questionnaires, surveys, telephone, or interview:

- Name:
- Size (Total number of user base):

- Role:
- Experience:
- Training:
- Cultural Values:
- Learning Style:
- Age:

2. Analyze the task:

1. What is the function of this icon?
2. Why do this task?
3. When to do this task?
4. Steps in the procedure
5. Required resources (e.g. software)
6. Result of the task

3. Determine the appearance and interaction (look at Alternatives):

Name   Alternative Description

-------   -----------------------
-------   -----------------------

4. Use pencil and paper to draw black and white prototype alternatives:

Alternative Sketches for an Icon Representing Creativity
(Horton, 1994)

5. Seek users' preference
6. Refine and colorize, then scan
7. Iteration and test with users: After an icon has been designed for the first time, test with users to see if the see the intended meaning is clear. If users interpretations do not comply with the intended meaning of the icon, then change and revise the icon so that the user readily interprets its meaning.

Chapter 8
Animation, Video, and Audio

Animation, video, and audio are dynamic building blocks for e-learning, and their impact on education and training is huge. However, because the very nature of these media requires a lot of downloading time, we must be very careful in how we use them. The real challenge in using these glamorous technologies is to integrate them into e-learning environments to increase the educational outcome of the site. Some developers get carried away and place these technologies on their Web sites or their CD-ROMs for no other reason, but to show off the power of these technologies.

In this chapter, I will discuss these media as they are incorporated into e-learning. To achieve this goal I will first discuss the essential features of authoring tools that allow developers to incorporate animation, sound, and video on their e-learning site. I will then provide an introduction to Macromedia *Flash MX*, as the authoring tool of choice, whose features support incorporation of animation, sound, and video for e-learning. To achieve these goals I will discuss the following topics:

- Essential Features of Authoring Tools for Animation, Sound, and Video
- Macromedia Flash MX (henceforth Flash)
- Basic Elements of Flash
  - o Toolbox
  - o Timeline
  - o Library
  - o Stage
- Authoring Procedure for Flash
  - o Developing an Idea
  - o Creating objects
  - o Placing Objects on the Stage and the Timeline
  - o Creating Animation

- o   Writing ActionScript for Navigation, and Interactivity.
- Working with Sound
- Importing Sounds into Flash
- Working with Video
  - o   Capture a Video
  - o   Editing the Video
  - o   Incorporate the Video into Flash
- Publishing Flash movies for E-learning Sites.

Essential Features of Authoring Tools for Animation, Sound, and Video

Authoring tools for animation come in a variety of categories and different levels of authoring. Because of the diverse nature of these authoring systems, some of them may not meet the requirements and the demands of educators or developers. In what follows, information about some features of authoring tools for animation, sound, and video production that are most suitable for developing e-learning is provided.

Authoring tools for animation are packaged with a variety of features such as interactivity, video and audio support, scripting, and compression. Authoring tools for creating animation, sound, and video should have, at the minimum, the following features: organizational view, editors, scripting, interactivity, playback, and publishing capability.

1. *Organizational View*: Animation for e-learning productions generally involves a series of events. These events are presented with components of multimedia such as text and graphics, and they are carefully incorporated together with the aid of authoring tools to create animation. During production, the events as well as the timing and synchronization of different components of the multimedia are routinely checked.

Authorware, for example, provides a flowchart of related icons that displays the relationship of events and other components of a production. Flash uses a spreadsheet like feature, called a Timeline, to show a time-based display of the events and synchronization of the different components of the multimedia. Authoring tools that provide some kind of mechanism to display the overall view of the multimedia production are highly recommended.

2. *Editing tools*: There are hundreds of editing tools available that can create and edit images, video and audio. For example, Photoshop is an excellent imaging tool, Premiere and *Final Cut Pro* are the most widely used video editing software, and SoundEdit and Sound Forge are ideal for editing sound. Fortunately some authoring tools are bundled with editing tools for text, graphics, and sound. In most cases, the editing tools that are included with the authoring tools are sufficient for a medium range multimedia production. In selecting authoring tools, the rule of thumb is that the more editors an authoring tool has the more convenient and cost effective the system. For example, Director and Flash are bundled with a graphics program, sound, and text manipulation editors. Most authoring tools are more than capable of importing the majority of file types for sound, video, and graphics

3. *Scripting*: The major problem with authoring tools is that the finer features of interactive multimedia during production are not in the control of the producer. The flow of the production is dictated by the authoring tools, and the program makes most of the decisions. To avoid this limitation and to provide more control for the developers, the majority of authoring tools are bundled with a scripting language. Scripting provides more interactive power and more precise control during production. Authoring tools like Director, Flash, ToolBook, and Authorware are all equipped with some kind of scripting language. These languages may be called by different names such as Lingo for Director, OpenScript for ToolBook or ActionScript for Flash. However, their primary purpose is to provide more control over the development of the finer points of interactive multimedia.

Scripting is in fact a programming language. However, it resembles English lexicon and syntax. Most commands and functions in scripting languages are easily understood by most people. Such English-like features allow most educators to write their own scripting, which optimizes the production. In selecting an authoring tool to create animation, sound, and video for e-learning, educators and developers need to carefully consider the scripting capabilities of the software they are going to use.

4. *Playback*: During production, developers of animation, sound, and video for e-learning must constantly and continually look at what has been produced. It is not unusual for an animation piece to be tested and retested hundreds of times during production. Authoring tools must have a convenient and easy way to make going back and forth between production and display a relatively easy task.

Another aspect of playback that relates to post production time and distribution is the ability of the user to play back the piece without relying on the original software. Some systems allow the user to play back the production without worrying about the platform or specific software. For example, Director allows the developer to create a projector from the piece. Such projectors allow the playback feature of the production in the absence of the original. Another example is the runtime in Authorware that allows packaging the multimedia piece without relying on the original application. When educators wish to select an authoring tool for production, it is essential to carefully consider the relative ease of the playback feature for both during and post production.

Macromedia Flash MX

Flash has been around for several years. Like other software, Flash has gone through several versions. Originally it was called *Future Splash* till Macromedia bought it. It was then called Flash with specific versions (e.g. Flash 5). The latest version is called Flash MX.

In recent years Flash has come to be extremely popular among educators. The popularity of Flash is due to several factors. First, it is one of the most powerful authoring systems that include all the essential features of authoring tools. These features enable educators to have control on the minutest elements during the process of animation production. Another factor that has added to Flash's popularity is its flexibility, which provides educators the ability to create stand alone applications that can be distributed to other users. Probably the most salient factor that has contributed to Flash's popularity is its compatibility with the Web.

Flash as an authoring tool allows its users to create animation with sound, graphics, and interactivity, which are called movies. During a typical project, you create objects in the library using various tools that are included in Flash. Then you bring the object from the library onto the stage and animate it along the Timeline. To add interactivity, you use ActionScript to create buttons and sophisticated animation. You preview the movie by using the controller to test the movie. If you are happy with your movie, you can either publish it as a stand alone movie or publish as .SWF (Shock Wave Flash) file to be used on the Internet as part of your e-learning project.

This section will provide the reader with a clear understanding of the elements of Flash, and the skills to author interactive movies and write some basic ActionScript. Once the reader has a firm grasp of the basic elements of Flash, I will discuss how you can import sound and video into a Flash movie. Experimentation with Flash is highly recommended to discover the marvels that come with the program.

Basic Elements of Flash

Flash movies are actually like a series of stages where the developer places animation, sound, video, special effects, and buttons for interactivity. These stages are interwoven. When you open the Flash program you will notice some open elements of Flash similar to Figure 8.1. If the library is not open when you first start Flash, use the Window menu and then select Library. There are many elements of Flash that play essential roles in creation of a movie. However, there are only four of them that are absolutely necessary to create movies. These windows are: Toolbox, Timeline, Stage, and Library.

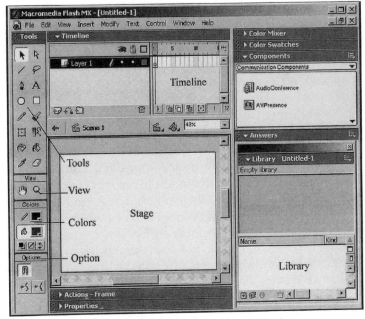

Figure 8.1 Basic Elements of Flash

Toolbox

The Toolbox can be used to create lines, rectangles, circles, fill in color, select objects, and other basic functions of a vector-based graphics program. Figure 8.2 illustrates that the Toolbox has four sections:

1. The Tools section has a variety of tools for selecting objects, drawing objects, color fill, line fill, and transforming objects.
2. The View section contains tools to magnify or move the view of the Stage.
3. The Colors section has a color palette to work with colors for strokes and fill.
4. The Options section shows modifiers for a selected tool.

Timeline

The timeline window records and plays all actions of objects including the location of graphics on stage, the timing of sounds, the ActionScript, etc. The timeline is very much like the brain of Flash that guides and monitors every action of a Flash movie.

Figure 8.2 shows the Timeline with three layers. You can add layers to the Timeline by clicking on its button in the lower left. The Timeline is laid out as a grid, very similar to a spreadsheet with rows and columns. The intersection of a row and a column is called a frame, which contains information about the objects, sounds, colors, graphics, text, video, etc. A frame represents a single moment in a Flash movie. It is a snapshot of everything you see on a stage for a moment.

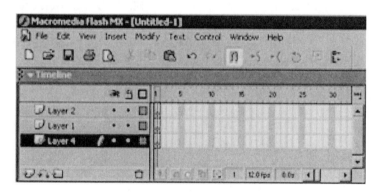

Figure 8.2 The Timeline

There is also a rectangular red head that serves as a playback mechanism. Very much like the playback head on a VCR, it determines the specific moments in each frame. When you play a movie, the Timeline moves from one frame to the next, the playback head reads the information in each frame, and then carries out the special directions the Flash program is dictating.

Frames by themselves reveal no animation. However, when frames are placed in a horizontal sequence, Flash creates animation that looks alive. In order to make the animation happen, each frame must have a keyframe. To make a frame into a keyframe you should select Insert > Keyframe.

Library

Any digitized object can be stored in the Library. These objects can be symbols, buttons, or a movie Clip. Symbols include graphics, text, sound, music, voice, *QuickTime* movies, etc. There are two approaches to develop symbols: create inside in the Library or import them into the Library.

If the Library is not open, you must select Window > Library. To create a symbol in the library, you can select Insert > New Symbol. The Library and its New Symbol editing stage automatically open up. Note that the editing stage for the Library is different than the normal stage in Flash. The difference is indicated by a (+) in the center of the editing stage for the Library. You create objects, such as graphics or text, using such tools as a pencil, brush, eraser, etc. in the Toolbox.

You can also import graphics, sound, and QuickTime animation created in many other applications. To import graphics, sound, video, etc. into the Library, please select File > Import. Then find the item that you wish to import and click on Open. The selected item is automatically imported into your Library.

Stage

The Stage is the area where most elements of animation such as graphics or text are placed. Unlike other Windows in Flash, the Stage is always present and acts as the placeholder within which all Flash movies are played. Generally the Stage covers the entire screen; however, the size of the Stage can be set by selecting Modify > Document and then indicating the width and the height of the document.

During production of a movie, objects from the Library are dragged onto the Stage for accurate positioning. Flash places a copy of the object on the Stage. However, there are several objects such as audio and ActionScript that have no physical appearance on the stage. These types of objects are placed in the

Timeline window, and they perform their function in the appropriate frame that the developer decides.

The objects that are placed on the Stage are referred to as Instances. Object members and Instances may appear to be identical, but they are not. The original object member always stays the same. However, when an object is dragged onto the Stage, Flash actually places a copy of that object on the Stage. This is an important distinction. An object from the Library can have more than one Instance on the Stage. For example, an image in the Library that has been placed onto the Stage can be resized in one frame, or be placed in a different position in another frame, and so on. This ability of creating different Instances from the same object has important implications for animation, as well as saving precious memory on the computer that is running the animation on the Web.

Authoring Procedure for Flash

To demonstrate the authoring procedure in Flash, we shall build a movie that has a very simple animation with interactivity. Regardless of how simple or complicated a movie may be, authoring in Flash involves several universal steps:

1. Developing an Idea
2. Creating Objects
3. Placing Objects on the Stage and the Timeline
4. Creating Animation.
5. Writing ActionScript for Navigation, and Interactivity.

Developing an Idea

Creating a movie in Flash, like developing any other e-learning project, is a cyclical process that starts with an idea. When the idea for a movie is being developed, at least three guidelines must be considered:

1. Understand your users before creating a movie.
2. Decide on the subject matter of your movie, and what it wants to accomplish.

3. If your movie is interactive, plan an effective navigation throughout your movie. Avoid complicated and confusing interactivity.

Using pencil and paper, storyboard the overall design of the idea, and sketch out the screen design. In the simple interactive animation we are going to build, the idea is that a circular object can roll across a line. The Stage with two buttons (Roll and Back), a ball, and a line is first sketched. The pencil and paper drawing will look something like Figure 8.3.

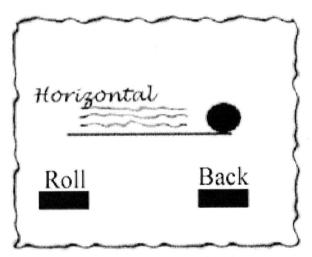

Figure 8.3 Sketch the Animation

Creating Objects

For the purpose of the simple animation in this section, we shall first create four objects in the Library. Open Macromedia Flash and choose Insert > New Symbol. Figure 8.4 shows the dialog box for Create New Symbol. Make sure Graphic is selected, name the new symbol Line and then click OK. The Library automatically opens with the editing stage.

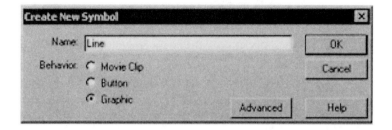

Figure 8.4 Dialog Box for New Symbol

Follow the steps below to create four simple images in the Library:

1. Select the line tool.
2. Click and drag while holding down the shift key to draw a horizontal line about six inches. (Do not worry about the exact measurement.)
3. Make sure the Library is open. Click on the Add button that is located at the bottom left side in the Library. The Add New Symbol button creates a new dialog box. Name the new symbol Ball and then click OK.
4. Select the Oval tool.
5. On the Editing Stage for New Symbol, click and drag to draw a circle about a half-inch by half-inch. (Do not worry about the exact measurement.)
6. Using the Fill Color palette, select a red color.
7. Select the Bucket tool from the Toolbox, and click inside the ball to make it red.
8. Click on the Add New Symbol button in the Library. Click on the Graphic button and name it Roll.
9. Select the Text tool. Then, choose 18 points for the size of text from the Text Property.
10. Select the Text tool and click and drag slightly in the editing area, then type Roll.
11. Click on the Add New Symbol button in the Library.

12. Select the Text tool. Then, choose 18 points for the size of text from the Text Property.
13. Click in the Stage editing area and drag slightly, then type Back.
14. Note that there are four new objects in the Library window.
15. Select Edit > Edit Document to go back to the main Stage. Note that there are no objects on the main Stage because we have not moved any objects from the Library yet.
16. Choose (Save As ...) from the File menu.
17. Type Roll for the movie's name.
18. Then click OK.

Placing Objects on the Stage and the Timeline

Objects from the Library can be placed in a Flash movie by clicking and dragging them to the exact position desired on the Stage. To place the objects you made in the previous section onto the Stage of the Roll movie follow the steps below:

1. Open the Flash Movie called Roll. Then, open the Library by selecting Window > Library.
2. Click on the Insert Layer button (As shown in Figure 8.5) four times.
3. Double click on the top layer and type in Line as its name (As shown in Figure 8.5).
4. Repeat naming other layers as Ball, Roll, and Back. (As shown in Figure 8.5).
5. Click in the first frame of the layer Line. This is where the first object (line) will be recorded.
6. In the Library, find the object you previously called Line. Click on the line and drag it onto the Stage. (As shown in Figure 8.5).
7. Click in frame 1 of the layer Ball. This is where the object (Ball) will be recorded.
8. Click on the Ball object in the Library and place it on the Stage slightly above the right side of the line. (As shown in Figure 8.5).

9. Click in frame 1 of the layer Roll. This is where the text object Roll will be recorded.
10. Click on the text object Roll in the Library and drag it onto the Stage to be placed slightly below the horizontal line. (As shown if Figure 8.5).
11. Click in frame 1 of the layer Back. This is where the text object Back will be recorded
12. Click on the text object (Back) in the Library and drag it onto the Stage to be placed slightly below the horizontal line. (As shown in Figure 8.5).
13. This is a good time to save your movie.

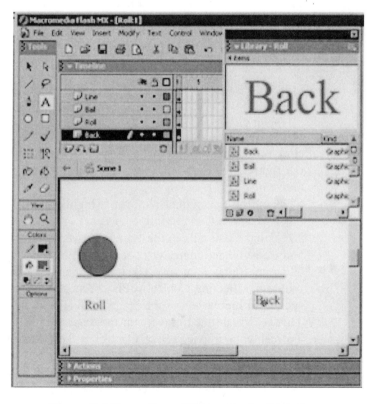

Figure 8.5 Recording of Object in the Timeline

Creating Animation

Flash allows creation of several different animations. Two of the most useful types of animation are tweening and frame-by-frame animation. The fundamental principle for these types of animation is cell animation. To demonstrate, we shall use tweening animation in this section. Follow the steps below to create tweening animation that allows the ball to roll on the stage:

1. In the Timeline window, click on frame 60 in the Line layer. Press Shift on the keyboard, and hold while clicking on frame 60 in the Back layer. Note that all four frames in column 60 are highlighted.
2. Select Insert > Frame to include frames for all layers up to frame 60.
3. In the Timeline, click in frame 60 of the Ball layer.
4. Select Insert > Keyframe to insert a key frame in frame 60 of the Ball layer.
5. While frame 60 in the Ball layer is still highlighted, click on the ball on the Stage, drag it all the way to the right of the horizontal line, and place it slightly above it.
6. Click on frame 1 in the Ball layer to highlight.
7. Select Insert > Create Motion Tween.
8. Note, that Flash fills in the frames between frame 1 and frame 60 and indicates tweening by an arrow.
9. Click in frame 1 of any layer, and then play the movie by selecting Control > Play. You should first see the ball move across the Stage on the line.
10. This is a good time to save your movie.
11. To test your movie, select Control > Test Movie. You should see a new Window opening and playing your movie. Note that Testing your movie is actually the same as saving the Flash movie as Flash.fla, which can be a stand alone movie that anyone can play regardless of whether they have Flash or not.

A ball rolling on a line may not be a very impressive animation. However, this type of animation is called cell animation, which is the basis of even the most sophisticated animation that is produced by Disney or Warner Brothers. Except they do frame by frame animation; whereas, here Flash filled in all the frames for you. It is possible to do frame by frame animation in Flash, as you move the ball in each frame, but each frame must be converted into a Keyframe. The power of animation in Flash, however, comes from Tweening animation and writing ActionScript for interactivity.

Writing ActionScript for Navigation and Interactivity

Writing ActionScript may at first appear daunting; however, once the reader gets used to it and discovers the hidden power of ActionScript, it becomes a routine procedure. Here, we shall discuss a few ActionScript commands, and show how they can be used to create buttons and interactivity.

One of the most useful components of Flash is creating buttons that allow the developer to create interactivity with ActionScript. Buttons in Flash are created the same way as creating graphics in Insert > New Symbol. To create buttons for your movie Roll:

1. Open a new Flash document.
2. Select Insert > New Symbol.
3. In the dialog box make sure Button is selected.
4. Give a new name to your button (e.g. Button 1)
5. Click OK.

Note that when the Editing Stage for button opens there are only four frames in the Timeline. These four frames are Up, Over, Down, and Hit as shown in Figure 8.6. It is important to understand the functions of these four frames.

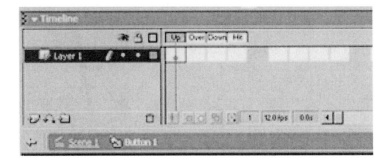

Figure 8.6 Four States of Button

Here is a brief description of these four frames:
1. UP: This frame is the normal holding for the image that will be displayed on the stage.
2. Over: When the end user moves the mouse over the button in a Flash movie, this frame displays the second image, text, or animation.
3. Down: This is the third image, which is triggered when the end user clicks the mouse on the button.
4. Hit: This is the hot spot. When the button is released, this area becomes active to do what the button is supposed to do. For example if the button has the ActionScript to get a URL for a Web site, then this action is performed.

Follow the steps below to make a button for our movie Roll:

6. Open the Flash Movie called Roll if it is not already open.
1. Select Insert > New Symbol.
2. In the Dialog box make sure Button is selected.
3. Call your button Button1 and then click OK.
4. In the Button Editing Stage, click on the frame Up to highlight if it is not already highlighted.

5. Select a rectangle tool from the Toolbox and draw a rectangle on the Editing Symbol Stage approximately one inch by two inches.

6. Choose green from the Paint Palette.

7. Select the Paint Bucket, click on the rectangle on the Editing Stage to change the color to green.

8. Click the frame Over to highlight.

9. Select Insert > Keyframe.

10. Note that the rectangle from frame Up is copied into the frame Over.

11. Choose red from the Paint Chip. Select the paint bucket.

12. With the bucket still selected, click on the rectangle to change the color to red.

13. Click on the frame Down to highlight it.

14. Select Insert > Keyframe.

15. Note that the rectangle from frame Over is copied into the frame Down.

16. Select the paint bucket. Choose blue from the Paint Palette.

17. With the bucket still selected, click on the rectangle on the editing stage to change the color to blue.

18. Click the frame Hit to highlight.

19. Select Insert > Keyframe.

20. Note that the rectangle from frame Down is copied into the frame Hit.

21. Select the paint bucket. Choose black from the Paint Chip.

22. With the bucket still selected, click on the rectangle to change its color to black.

23. Select Edit > Edit Document to get back to the main stage for the document. Note that in the Library you now have a new object called Button 1.

24. This is a good time to save your movie.

Now write some ActionScript. First, you want the animation to stay in the first frame.

1. Select Insert > Layer to create a new layer in your movie.
2. Double click in the new Layer and type in Buttons for its name.
3. Select Frame 1 in the Button layer to highlight it.
4. Select Window > Action. The ActionScript dialog box appears.
5. Click on the (+) then select Action > Movie Control > Stop. (See Figure 8.7)
6. Select Frame 60 in the Buttons layer to highlight it.
7. Select Insert > Keyframe.
8. While still in Keyframe 60, select Window > Action. The ActionScript dialog box appears.
9. Click on the (+) then select Action > Movie Control > Stop. (See Figure 8.7)
10. This is a good time to save your movie.

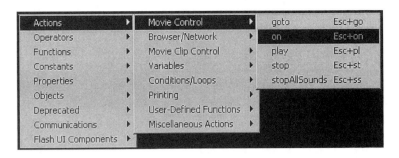

Figure 8.7 Adding ActionScript

Note that if you Test the movie now, it will not play like before because you have asked it to stop on Frame 1 by inserting ActionScript for it function. Now let's bring two buttons on the stage to make the movie play as follow:

1. Open the Movie Roll if it is not already open.
2. Click on the First frame in the Layer called Buttons.
3. Select Window > Library.
4. In the Library find the button you named Button 1.

5. Click and drag Button 1 onto the Stage and place it slightly above the text Roll. (See Figure 8.8)

6. Click on Button 1 on the Stage to highlight it.

7. Select Window > Action.

8. In the Action Dialog Box click on the (+) then select Action > Movie Control > Play.

9. Close the Action Dialog Box.

10. Click and drag Button 1 from the Library onto the Stage again, and place it slightly above the text Back. See (Figure 8.8)

11. In the Action Dialog Box click on the (+), then select Action > Movie Control > Goto.

12. Once you select Goto, a new dialog box appears. (See Figure 8.8)

13. Leave everything as it is. Make sure the frame number is 1.

14. Close the ActionScript Dialog Box.

15. This is a good time to save you movie.

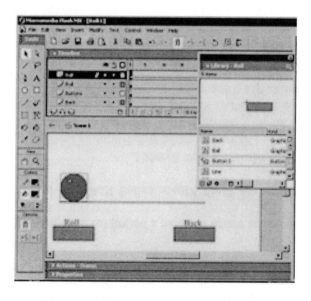

Figure 8.8 Placing Buttons on the Stage

Test your movie by selecting Control > Test Movie. Although the movie is playing, everything appears at first to be still, and it looks like nothing is happening. You will see all your objects as you had placed them on the Stage. However, the reason why it appears that nothing is happening is because of the ActionScript you wrote for this frame is to stop. If you click on the Roll button, you will notice that the ball moves across the Stage. This is because you wrote an ActionScript for the button Roll to play. The circle rolls sixty frames and then stops on Frame 60. This is because you wrote another ActionScript to stop on Frame 60. If you click on the Back button, the ball rolls back on the Stage and stops on Frame 1. This is because you wrote an ActionScript command for it to stop on frame 1.

Working with Sound

Sound is one of the most effective media that can be embedded into an e-learning site. In some cases such as foreign language teaching, reading, and directions on sites for the blind, sound becomes absolutely essential. In most cases sound is more powerful than text. Sound may be used for speech, music, or special effect. The main issues are how can we find the appropriate source to import sound and what sound formats do browsers support.

The source for a sound to be imported into an e-learning site may be analog. In the case of an analog source, it must first be converted into a digital format. To convert an analog source into digital material, you must use an analog to digital converter. This process requires the use of specialized hardware as well as software.

Today, most digital sources come from CD-ROMs, and can be captured by the use of specialized software such as *SoundEdit* for Macintosh or *Sound Forge* for Windows. Once sound is imported into the software, it can be manipulated and edited. It can also be imported into authoring tools such as Flash. Although some authoring tools such as Flash allow some editing, they are not powerful enough for sophisticated editing.

The other issue in using sound for e-learning is its formats. At the present time the two popular browsers are

Netscape and Explorer. Netscape reads MIDI, WAV, AU, and AIFF formats. Explorer reads AU, SND, WAV, AIFF, AIF, and AIFC files. Of course there are a few more formats; however, these are the sound extensions formats that today's popular browsers support. One of the most recent technologies for sound, especially as it relates to the Web, is the MP3 format. MP3, which stands for Moving Picture Experts Group, Audio Layer III, is a process that compresses audio files that keeps the integrity of the original sound. If the original integrity is kept intact, then the quality of sound is much better than other compressed sounds that do not keep their original integrity. Because of its quality, wide availability, and its small size, MP3 is wonderful for use in Flash and e-learning sites.

Importing Sounds into Flash

Flash recognizes three kinds of audio formats *.WAV* (Window), *AIFF* (Macintosh), and *MP3* for both platforms. However, if you have QuickTime installed on your system, Flash will support the majority of sound formats including *Sound Design II* (Macintosh), *System 7 Sounds* (Macintosh), Sound Only QuickTime Movies (Macintosh), *Sun AU* (Macintosh and PC), *AIFF* (Macintosh and PC), and WAV (Macintosh and PC). In addition to these sound formats, Flash supports two kinds of sounds for use over the Internet: streaming sounds and event sounds. Streaming sounds begin playing when sufficient sound data has been downloaded as the rest of the data for sound streams in. Streaming gives the impression to the user that the sound has already been downloaded and they do not have to wait. Streaming is great for background music or continuous speech. Events are played when the entire sound has been downloaded. To import sound into a Flash environment:

1. Select File > Import. The Dialog Box for import appears.
2. Find the sources of sound in the Import Dialog Box and click Open. (If you do not have a sound source on your Desktop, please skip this section and go to the next section that deals with importing sound from within Flash.)

3. The imported sound is automatically added to the Library of your Flash movie.
4. Save your movie.

Sounds can also be imported from within Flash. To import sound from within Flash:

1. Open the Flash Movie called Roll.
2. Select Window > Common Library > Sound.
3. The Common Library of Flash for Sound opens. Click on Beam Scan and drag the sound into the Stage.
4. The sound has been imported into your movie. To see that the Beam Scan has been imported into your movie, select Window > Library. You will see the imported sound in your Library.
5. Save your movie.

To add sound to the Flash movie Roll:

1. Open the Flash movie Roll.
2. Open the Library and select Window > Library > Beam Scan.
3. Select Insert > Layer to add a new layer to your movie.
4. Double click on the new layer and call it Sound.
5. Click on the first frame of the layer Sound to highlight it if it is not already highlighted.
6. Click on Beam Scan in the Library and drag it onto the Stage.
7. You will notice that the sound has been added to the Timeline of the Sound layer.
8. Save your movie.
9. Select Control > Test Movie.
10. You will hear the sound play as the movie is being played.

Guidelines for Sound

- Quality of original sound is very important.
- Use sound to capture students' attention.
- Use sound effects to focus students' attention.
- Use speech for specialized courses such as teaching a foreign language.
- Use speech for students who may have difficulty reading.
- Users should be in control of sounds (e.g. turn it off).
- Be consistent in using sound in the Web site. Do not just use it once and then abandon its usage.

Working with Video

Digitized video has come to be an important part of e-learning. Videos can be used for instruction in a variety of ways. Because of its file size, using videos created numerous problems for the Web. However, in recent years with advances in hardware and software technology, using digitized video to teach has become more popular. In order to embed a video in an e-learning site you need to take the following steps:

- Capture the video
- Edit the video
- Incorporate the video into Flash

Capture the Video

Traditionally, capturing a video was performed from an analog source. To convert these analog videos into a digitized format, specialized hardware and software were required. One traditional approach was to connect a VCR to a video card of a computer and use specialized software such as *Premiere* or Final Cut Pro to carry out the conversion. With advances in video technology, it is now easier to capture a video on digitized video cameras such as those offered by Sony.

Editing the Video

Once the digitized video source is available, there are a huge number of software that allow editing it. Some of these software are *iMovie*, Final Cut Pro 3, and Premiere. As a general rule a professional should do the editing. However, for nonprofessionals, I think iMovie from Apple is an excellent beginners' level software to edit and embed the final form on the Web.

Incorporating Video into Flash

One of the easiest ways to incorporate video into an e-learning site is to use Flash. Originally Flash did not support video. However, with the introduction of Flash MX, it now supports Macromedia Flash Video (FLV) format files. In fact if you have QuickTime installed on your system, Flash will support videos with the following extensions: AVI, MPEG, MOV. To import video into Flash MX, you should do the following:

1. Select File > Import.
2. The import Dialog Box appears. Locate the video you wish to import
3. If your video is a MOV. or QuickTime, Flash will ask you if you want to embed or link the video to import. Select Embed if the video size is small and Link if the size of the video is large. If you choose embed the video, a video Setting Box appears
4. In the import Video Setting Box, select the appropriate quality, keyframe interval, and scale you wish. Remember, the higher the quality the larger the size of the video. Leave all other parameters as they are.
5. Click OK. Flash MX goes through the process of importing the video.
6. Test your movie and then save it.

Publishing Flash Movies for E-learning Sites

Flash publishes your movie in its default .swf format. It further can embed the published movie in an HTML document, which can be used on the Web. Flash also allows you to preview the published setting. If you wish to alter the default published setting, choose the File > Publish Setting. As illustrated in Figure 8.9, the setting for Format, Flash, and HTML can be altered. For the purpose of this brief introduction to Flash MX, leave all the settings for Publish as default, and then click on Publish.

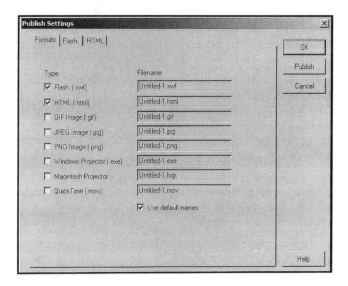

Figure 8.9 Publish Setting for Flash

To publish directly without changing the setting: choose File > Publish. Flash automatically burns a .SWF format of your movie and embeds it in an HTML document. It is essential that you know in which folder your original movie was saved because Flash publishes your movie and the HTML document in the same folder as the original movie.

Reflection

Before closing this chapter, it is important to note that Flash has a lot of advantages and a few disadvantages. The first advantage of Flash is the file size of the movies, which is extremely small in comparison to other animation created with other authoring tools. Small File size makes Flash an ideal tool for the Web. The second advantage of Flash is that it provides total control of the entire production to the developer. Flash movies are only limited by the imagination of their creator. Simple animation to highly complex multimedia titles can be created with Flash's powerful animation and ActionScript capabilities. Flash is also bundled with a very powerful graphics program. The graphics program in Flash actually rivals some of the other programs. One of the disadvantages of Flash is its learning curve. At first, it appears to be simple; however, in creating more sophisticated movies, Flash becomes difficult to master especially when it comes to placing complex ActionScript. Nevertheless, I believe that after getting used to the Flash environment, it becomes most enjoyable to use.

The reader should be reminded that because of Flash's extensive and powerful features, in as short a chapter as the present one, it will not be possible to discuss all the features Flash MX has to offer. However, the purpose of this chapter was to introduce the reader to the wonderful world of animation, sound and audio. I used Flash as a vehicle to carry out the goal of the chapter. To do justice to Flash, the following is a list of books that I would recommend for various levels of expertise in working with Flash:

Easy:
Chun, Russell. (2002) *Macromedia Flash MX advanced for Windows and Macintosh Visual QuickPro guide.* Berkeley: Macromedia Press.
Ulrich, Katherine & Chun, Russell. (2002). *Macromedia Flash MX for Windows and Macintosh: Visual QuickStart guide.* Berkeley: Macromedia Press

Intermediate:
Brumbaugh-Duncan, Cheryl. (2002). *The Flash MX project.* Indianapolis: New Riders.
Sahlin, Doug (2002) *Macromedia Flash(R) MX virtual classroom.* Berkeley: McGraw Hill.

Advance:

Kerman, Phillip. (2002) *ActionScripting in Flash MX.* Indianapolis: New Riders

Sanders, Bill. (2001). *Flash ActionScript f/x and design.* Scottsdale: Coriolis Group, LLC.

Chapter Nine
Page Layout and Site Architecture

Thus far in this book you have learned how learning theories can assist one to develop e-learning environments, how perceptual theories can aid in the design of interfaces, and how the basic elements of visual design play their roles. Two additional concepts that will help bring these elements together to create cohesive e-learning sites are page layout and site architecture. E-learning environments are made up of two components: individual pages, and the overall organization and relationship of these pages. Page layout focuses on how perceptual theories can assist in the proper arrangement of the basic elements of design on individual pages. The second aspect of e-learning design is to provide a systematic infrastructure that supports the content. Such an infrastructure that is concerned with dividing the content into smaller modules to be presented on the individual pages of a site is called site architecture. The purpose of this chapter is to discuss how to plan and develop a simple and elegant page layout, and how to create effective site architecture for e-learning. To achieve these goals this chapter will include the following topics:

- Page Layout Elements
  - o Proportion
  - o Grid lines to Assist Formatting a Page
  - o Alternative Sketches
  - o Guidelines for Page Layout
- Site Architecture
  - o Steps for Designing Site Architecture
    - Create Modules with Discrete Topics
    - Create Appropriate E-learning Site Architecture
      - Single Page Architecture
      - Sequential Architecture

- Hierarchical Architecture
- Grid Architecture
- Network Architecture
  - o   Guidelines for Site Architecture

Page Layout Elements

An experienced page layout professional is well aware of how to pull together the basic elements of design (e.g. text, images, color, animation, video) and establish a hierarchical relationship among these elements. A page layout professional is capable of establishing such a relationship and arrangement through his knowledge of scale, contrast, proportion, unity, harmony, grouping, and balance to create simple and elegant Web pages that are both functional and aesthetically pleasing. A well-designed Web page layout communicates information to the learner in a direct way.

For example, Figure 9.1 (a) and 9.1 (b) shows sketches for two different page layouts for the same amount of information for a fictitious e-learning site. The page layout in Figure 9 (a) shows the hierarchy of the global menu on the left and the local menu at the bottom through contrast of the size of the buttons and their placement. There is also a hierarchy of text size for the title, global menu, the local menu, and the content that communicates the importance of each element. There is also a logical grid layout for text and illustration. Figure 9 (b) shows the same kind of information. However, there seems to be an ad hoc layout of the elements of design that does not follow any knowledge of scale and contrast. The global menu has the same shape as the local menu. There is no hierarchy of prominence in regard to text size. There is no grid for text arrangements or the placement of the illustration. There is lack of scale use, inappropriate contrast, and absence of hierarchy, all of which make the layout of the page unappealing to the eye.

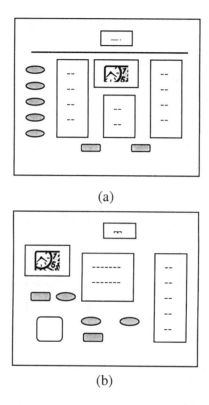

(a)

(b)

Figure 9.1 (a) and 1 (b)

Although both sketches in Figure 9 contain the same information, the one on the top (a) appears functional and the one on the bottom (b) appears confusing. The reason for the clarity in figure 9 (a) and confusion in 9(b) is that the former has followed some established principles for page layout and the latter did not. There are four principles that determine whether a page layout is effective or not. These principles are proportion, grid lines to assist formatting a page, alternative sketches, and designing pages.

Proportion

Proportion in design deals with the ratio between the elements of design. In the page layout process, proportion generally refers to the ratio of the length and the width of the pages. Throughout history, different cultures have used different proportions for printed materials and art. Looking at the history of print, there are four different relational proportions between the length and the width of printed pages. Figure 9.2 shows four typical proportions in design called a square, a natural rectangle, a golden rectangle, and a double square.

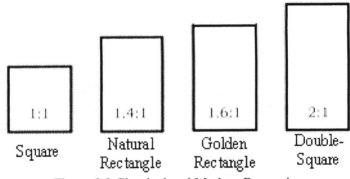

Figure 9.2 Classical and Modern Proportion

A square is an attention-getting proportion. It is generally used to indicate stability. It is not very common in book publishing or Web publishing as a proportion for each page; therefore, it is not recommended for e-learning pages. The natural rectangle, whose length is the square root of 2, and its width is 1, is ideal for traditional books and posters. It gives a natural feeling to the user. The golden rectangle has the unique property that an inscribed square leaves a remaining area whose sides are also of the golden rectangle proportion. The proportion of the length and the width for a golden rectangle is approximately 1.6 to 1, respectively. A double square is a rectangle made of two similar squares. This is the proportion that is used in Japanese art. Note, that the four different modern and classical proportions are not being used in the design of Web sites today. However, the proportion for the natural rectangle and golden rectangle may prove to be ideal for page layout on e-learning sites.

Grid Lines to Assist Formatting a Page

The majority of newspapers and other traditional printed materials use a grid to layout paper in their proportion. For example, newspapers are generally laid out in columns that are consistent on all pages. Figure 9.3 shows how traditional page designers layout their pages by using grids.

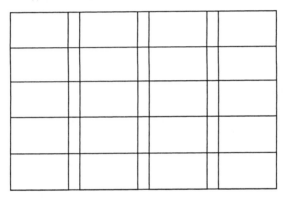

Figure 9.3 A Four-Column Grid

Grids are used as guides to align text, graphics, and other pertinent materials. In modern times, several page layout programs such as *PageMaker* or *Quark Xpress*, use the same grid procedure to layout pages for multimedia productions or brochure making. Grids in these applications are used to decide on the size of images and to help the viewer's eyes be guided to different areas of the page.

Using a grid to control Web page layout may prove to be slightly more difficult than traditional printed materials. The reason for this difficulty arises from the length and the width of default computer monitors (14 Inches) and the size of browsers such as Netscape or Explorer. As is shown in Figure 9.4, the proportion of a default browser is approximately 796 pixels for the width and 422 for the height. This makes deciding on the proportion of the page and the use of a grid a bit difficult because computer monitors are wider than they are taller. However, if we use the dimensions of a golden rectangle or a natural rectangle, then the columns of the grid must be flipped 90 degrees to approximately fit today's monitors and the size of the default browser.

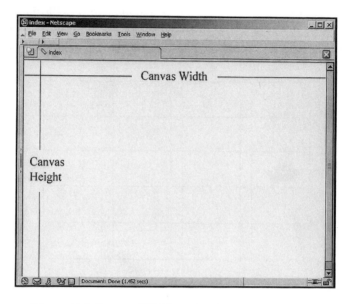

Figure 9.4 Canvas Width and Height for Netscape

To apply a grid to Web page layout, you must first determine the number of pixels that make up the length and the height of the visible area of the browser. Let's say the default number of pixels for the visible width of a browser is 480. Since I want to have a four-column grid, I first subtract 10 pixels from each side to account for the margin of the browser. I also wish to have 10 pixels between each column. (2X10+10X3=50). That leaves me with approximately 430 pixels for the width (480-50=430). If I Divide 430 by 4 the result is approximately 108 pixels that determines the width of each columns. I can do the same calculation for the height of the visible area of the default browser to get four rows. Using pencil and paper I then create a grid that has four columns and four rows. Figure 9.5 shows the grid for a page layout of four columns and four rows.

Figure 9.5 A Grid Layout with Four Columns and Four Rows

Alternative Sketches

Once the proportion and the grid has been determined, then using paper and pencil you should outline the placement for the elements of design such as the navigational system (global and local menus), text, images, video, and animation. At this stage, you should also determine the size of the text that establishes a hierarchy of importance. For example, text for title may be the largest with serif type, the global menu should be next in size, and then followed by the text size for the local menu and content text. Then you should sketch the page layout of the elements of design. In most instances, there should be several alternative sketches. Figure 9.6 shows a gird layout and one possible sketch for a layout process.

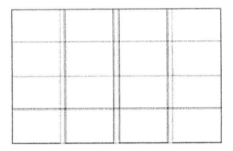

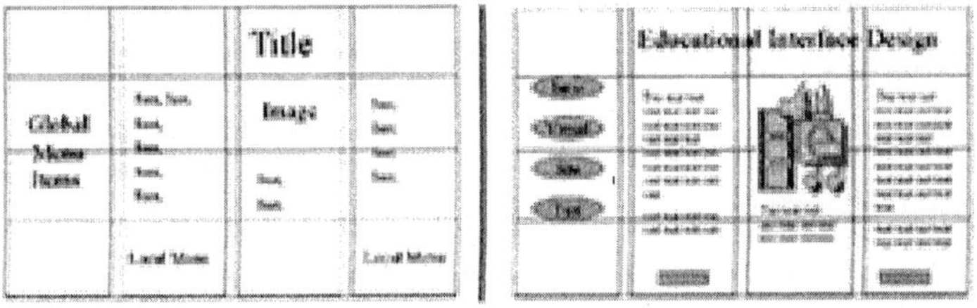

Figure 9.6 Grid Layout and One Possible Sketch

Once the alternative sketches have been prepared, they should be evaluated by several users/learners. The feedback you get from the learners/users should provide enough information for your best selection of page layout. A good Web editor, such as Macromedia *Dreamweaver*, or writing codes in HTML can help you to create tables or frames that would fit you page layout. These programs will help you to translate your grid division into a page layout for your site that is both functionally effective and aesthetically pleasing. Figure 9.7 shows how the grid layout has been translated into tables and what it looks like in Netscape browser.

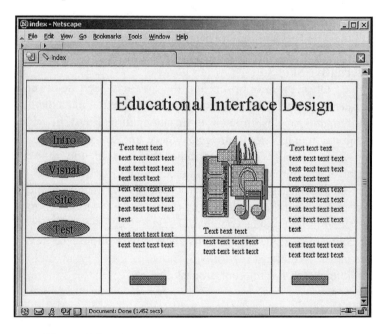

Figure 9.7 Using Tables or Frames for Page Layout

Guidelines for Page Layout
- Avoid excessive decorative text because it can be confusing and distract the user from finding real information.

- Design for the most common screen resolution and number of colors for your targeted user.
- Contrast has a strong effect on reading and comprehension.
- Use sufficient light and dark foreground and background.
- Test with typical users.
- Text and images on a low resolution screen are chunky or jagged. Use antialiasing to eliminate jagged resolution. We must be careful for it does not work with small text.
- Real estate on the screen is always at a premium. The only real solution is economy of presentation.
- Chunk information properly.
- The most effective way to align is to use a grid.
- Grab attention by visual weight such as color.
- Be consistent.
- Create a balanced visual appearance by the use of symmetry and appropriate white space.

Site Architecture

Organization is fundamental to human nature. We organize our schools both in a physical and administrative sense. Classrooms are organized to adhere to human behavior and for academic achievements. Educators and students even organize their binders for easy navigation and classifying information.

There are very few aspects of education that do not enjoy some kind of organization. The Web as an interactive educational tool is no exception in school settings. Organization of the Web into smaller units to represent content is called site architecture. Such organization concerns itself with the relationship among the Web pages that constitute the site. It also determines which pages precede the other, which has higher status, and which one acts as the main page.

In more traditional educational tools, such as a book or a video, students are used to sequential organization. They expect a beginning, a middle, and an end. The Web is a different kind of tool in that it can have the three fundamental levels of other educational tools, but does not necessarily follow sequential steps. It may have a beginning; however, there may be no end, or the middle may never come. Such a chaotic nature of the architecture of the Web may initially be preferred by the students. However, they often get lost or frustrated because they do not know where they are or where they are going.

At the subliminal level, all learners would like to be guided to a specific place on the Web. They may not admit to this fact. However, if the Web site is to act as an effective educational tool, its site architecture must be designed in a fashion that allows both constraint and discovery at the same time. Within such a guided discovery area, students must be able to navigate throughout an e-learning site with ease, and they must retain the information that is presented to them. One way to achieve such goals is to follow specific steps to design site architecture that adheres to the way students learn (See Part I).

Steps for Designing Site Architecture

A great majority of e-learning sites are designed by highly motivated, well intentioned, and intelligent educators who were in the rush to be on the Web. Most of these educators either bought a book on HTML or received a few hours of training on HTML, then rushed to place their curriculum on the Web. Such an urgency to be on the Web has resulted in creation of e-learning sites whose materials were originally designed for text-based instruction, but were directly placed on the Web. Such an insistence to place text-based materials on the Web has been responsible for educational sites that are in essence a long scrolling page. Long scrolling pages are not appropriate for the Web. After all, what is the purpose of a new tool if we are applying traditional standards in its design?

Another major problem of developing e-learning sites without much respect for careful planning and thorough research is the confusing site hyperlinks. Pages that are linked without regard for research and organization not only are harmful in themselves, but they generally lead students into endless browsing that makes them often forget where they are coming from or where they are going. Students generally get lost and confused in these chaotic organizations.

The careful e-learning designer must be aware and be sensitive to the architecture of the Web site that conforms to the limitations of the amount of content on each page and how these pages are linked to each other and external resources. Organization of material into manageable content and appropriate links are two important aspects of site architecture. There are two major steps in designing site architecture: create modules with discrete topics, and create appropriate e-learning site architecture.

Create Modules with Discrete Topics

In traditional text based writing, it is recommended that long and flowing passages be created where there is an introduction, body and conclusion. In the e-learning environment, such approach is not recommended. Students do not like to scroll down a window to read a long passage with introduction, body and conclusion. Instead, readers would like to see discrete topics where they can easily jump from one short topic to another. Therefore, in designing site architecture it is recommended to create appropriate site architecture that would display the topics, their relationship, their hierarchy, and their links.

In the chapters in Part I of this book, I discussed that content organization must follow the syntax of teaching models because such an order is based on the learning styles of the student. Basically, the syntax of any teaching model provides the Web designer with specific steps or a sequence for effective instruction. Each step in the syntax then becomes a series of instructional events. For example, in the teaching model for Mastery Learning, the second phase was to present the intended materials for instruction. Presenting the instructional materials for this phase as a continuous and scrollable text is not advisable for the Web. The first step is to consider subdividing the instructional materials into smaller units that are appropriate for the Web. Horton (1994) calls these smaller units for online publication Topics. Each Topic will provide the instructional content of different pages of a Web site.

Horton (1994) has provided the following suggestions for displaying topics online:

- Write discrete topics, not sprawling passages.
- Make each topic as complete as you can. Include or cross-reference all relevant related topics.
- Provide explicit pathways to related pieces of information, especially any necessary to understand the current topic.
- Do not depend on the user reading a long series of topics in a particular order.

For example, if you were to create an e-learning environment that is devoted to teaching an introduction to chemistry to middle school students, you would take the whole course and divide it into manageable modules. These modules would include such topics as what is matter made of, how are the elements arranged, what parts make up an atom, how are electrons arranged around the nucleus, how do compounds form, and so on. Each of these questions would become the topic of one module. The next step is to design the page layout, as discussed in the previous section, for each topic.

To use another example on how to create modules with discrete topics, let's say that you wish to create an online training program to teach PowerPoint. First you divide the whole lesson on PowerPoint into manageable modules. The modules for a course on PowerPoint could include these topics:

- How to Get Started?
- Working with Text
- Adding Graphics
- Working with Slides
- Working with Charts
- Selecting Lamination
- Running your Presentation

As before, the next step is to plan the page layout for each topic that would be appropriate to your audience.

Create Appropriate E-learning Site Architecture

There are a number of basic organizational patterns that site architecture can be organized around to allow learners to navigate throughout an e-learning site with ease and comfort. Horton (1994) has suggested four basic structures: sequential, hierarchical, grids, and web. Each one of these basic categories has their variants and the possibilities of combining them. These four basic patterns allow designers to select the most appropriate site architecture to adapt to the learners' educational needs. Several other publications (e.g. Apple Computer, Inc, 1989) have also proposed some structural organization for multimedia. They have used other terms to describe similar patterns of organization. In what follows I shall discuss five basic categories. These categories are similar to Horton's proposal (1994); however, they are not the same. These categories are

- Single Page Architecture
- Sequential Architecture
- Hierarchical Architecture
- Grid Architecture
- Network Architecture

Single Page Architecture

It is possible and sometimes preferable to have the main page of an e-learning site as the only page available to the reader. Such architecture is preferable when all activities are contained within one page. Sites that have single page architecture may consist of other windows or frames where additional information is displayed. However, the learner may not be aware of them.

With some knowledge of frames, *JavaScript* or multimedia software such as Director, Flash or imagemap, designers can create a single page e-learning site where all pertinent information can be displayed in a variety of ways as the learner explores different areas of the page.

For example, Figure 9.8 illustrates how the use of Flash and JavaScript allows creation of single page architecture. The content is the periodic table. It has been organized according to discovery models of teaching under guidance. Each chemical element represents a module or a topic. Each chemical element is also a button that was created using Flash. Within Flash, ActionScript has been used to talk to JavaScript for the main page to call up a pop up window. Clicking on the different chemical elements invokes a window where different topics represent the content describing particulars of that chemical element. Note that Figure 9.8 shows the topics for Helium after the user has clicked on the He button in the periodic table. Furthermore, in the pop-up window, the button will also dynamically present more information about that particular chemical element.

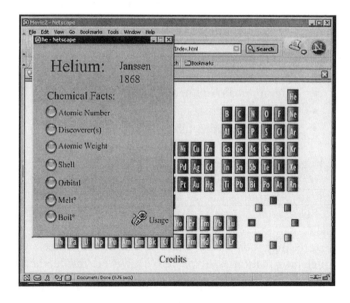

Figure 9.8 Single Page Architecture

Figure 9.9 shows another variation of single page architecture. This absolutely wonderful and elegant e-learning site uses frames and Flash to create single page architecture. The learner is not aware of the other resources that bring in information. However, the site uses Flash to create multimedia units in the right frame so that students can click on different topics to do research on the hazards of tobacco, alcohol, marijuana, and heroin. Once the learner clicks on one of the topics, such as smoking, they can choose its effect on the brain, lungs, heart, liver, and nervous system. As the learner clicks on different organs such as the brain or heart, relevant information is provided in the left frame. The learner never leaves the main page. However, an incredible amount of interactivity is provided on this single page architecture.

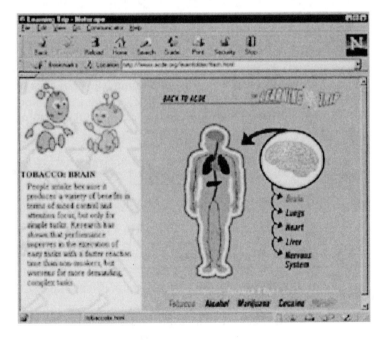

Figure 9.9 Variation of Single Page Architecture

Single page architecture is appropriate for displaying information when the learner is in control of choosing the topic for research. However, this type of architecture is most appropriate for discovery under guidance or the inquiry-teaching model that was discussed in Part I of this book. Although the learner has control over what they choose to discover, they cannot leave the site. This does not mean that other links cannot be provided, or that new addresses cannot be typed in to go to other sites. However, if the designer wishes to have some control, this type of site architecture is preferable.

Sequential Architecture

Sequential architecture is probably the closest to the more traditional structure of books. It has one logical sequence that is one page follows the next. It has a beginning and an end. In such architecture the learner is more or less guided by the design. There is very little choice for the learner.

Figure 9.10 illustrates that navigation in e-learning sites with sequential architecture can be forward or backward. It is perfectly acceptable to design an e-learning site that has just forward movement. However, such architecture generally should have a return to the main page available to the students. Figure 9.11 displays a looping architecture for a sequential structure.

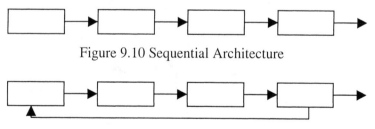

Figure 9.10 Sequential Architecture

Figure 9.11 Sequential with a Loop to the Main Page.

There are other variations of sequential Web structure. For example, a loop can be created so that the learner can navigate to the main page from any point. Figure 9.12 shows yet another alternative where side navigation is possible. However the overall navigation is still sequential.

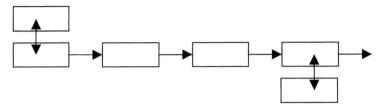

Figure 9.12 Sequential Architecture with Side Navigation

Sequential e-learning architecture is ideal for lessons that require a specific order or step-by-step instruction. Other usage of sequential architecture may be for presentation of drawings such as in a museum art gallery, slide shows such as in the national parks, a series of related images, a sequence such as a recipe, a chronological order such as historical events, a cause and effect such as heat expands length, or index ordering such as authors, books, or Web sites.

Sequential e-learning architecture works best in combination with other sequential architecture or other types of Web architecture. For example, in educational settings where zooming into a specific area is essential, one can design a display in greater detail. Imagine a geography lesson where one can zoom from Earth into California into the Bay Area to study the ecosystem of the bay.

Hierarchical Architecture

A hierarchical architecture allows the learner to choose from a variety of items and navigate to the path of choice. It is probably the closest type of architecture to the human mind and the fashion in which it operates. This type of structure has prevailed in a majority of human endeavors. We see hierarchical architecture in business, government, religion and schools. The Web is no exception.

Hierarchical architecture has come to dominate a majority of well designed e-learning sites. The simplest form of hierarchical architecture is tree architecture. Tree architecture allows creation of a menu on the main page where the user has explicit choice to branch down into the pages that are most relevant. Figure 9.13 shows a simple tree-like architecture that allows navigation into a sequential architecture. The learner can choose a specific path and then navigate within the sequential structure and return to the main page.

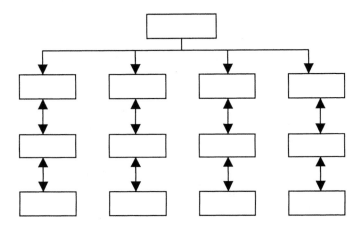

Figure 9.13 Sequential Architecture with Side Navigation

Hierarchical architecture can assume a variety of forms other than simple tree-like. For example, top-down hierarchy allows branching into the levels below the top. However, all items in different levels must contain the same type of information. For example, a school may create a Web site where the first level would be different departments. The next level below a department would be people (e.g. faculty and staff). The third level may be academics. However, each layer in such a hierarchy contains the same type of information.

One of the major concerns of designing hierarchical architecture is depth and breadth. Depth is referred to as the number of levels a site architecture can have. For example in Figure 9.13, there are three levels in addition to the main page. Breadth is defined as the number of menu items in each level. As a general rule depth should be no deeper than three levels. The breadth should also be no more than seven items (Schniederman 1992).

Hierarchical architecture is preferred when instruction can be subdivided into ordered hierarchies. For example, in part I of this book, I discussed several teaching models for content organization. The syntax of the teaching models can provide the subdivision of a hierarchy. Figure 9.14 shows how each menu item provides the link to the subdivision.

Figure 9.14 Virtual Skies
http://virtualskies.arc.nasa.gov/vsmenu/vsmenu.html

At first glance the subordinating goals are not immediately identifiable. However, mousing over each circular image on the orientation (or opening) page reveals the following subdivisions: Aviation Weather, Aviation Research, Airport Design, Air Traffic Management, Navigation, Communication, and Aeronautics. In Chapter Three, I discussed in detail how each subdivision has its own hierarchy below it.

Grid Architecture

Grid pattern architecture for e-learning is a series of rows and columns arranged to provide a convenient way to organize information. Grid patterns are extremely common to our daily lives. We play games (e.g. Chess) on grids, we live in cities where grids determine the patterns of streets, and we use tables to create rows and columns to organize information such as multiplication table.

The use of grid architecture for e-learning sites can become confusing if the arrangement is not properly designed. For example, Figure 9.15 shows a series of rows and columns representing the pages of an e-learning site. Such architecture allows navigation in horizontal sequences or vertical sequences. This type of architecture is ideal for e-learning sites that promote detailed explanation of a given topic.

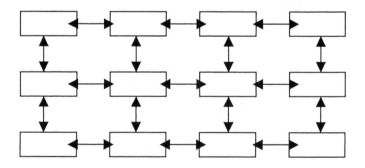

Figure 9.15 Shows Rows and Columns for a Grid

Network Architecture

Network architecture is sites that are arranged without any specific hierarchical or logical arrangement. It is similar to the structure of the Web as a whole where the learner can navigate to other topics for the purpose of discovering and learning new concepts. Figure 9.16 shows typical network architecture.

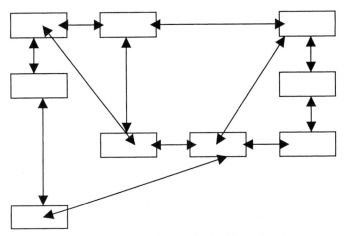

Figure 9.16 Typical Network Architecture.

The free nature of network architecture has some advantages and certain disadvantages. Its advantages come from the fact that e-learning sites can be arranged in any pattern and allow external links. This allows the learners to create their own way of learning. Such structure promotes learning by discovering and exploration new ideas. However, the danger of such a pattern may be that the developer links everything to everything else. At times there is no real educational purpose to the links, and learners end up confused and lost. They may become frustrated. Network architecture is ideal for the time when the learner is under the guidance of a teacher or a group with a specific assignment. This type of architecture may be ideal for cooperative learning and inquiry training models of teaching that were discussed in Part I of this book.

Guidelines for Site Architecture

- Remain consistent.
- Provide feedback if user is lost.
- Consider depth and breadth carefully.
- Offer alternatives for navigation.

- Require economy of action to navigate.
- Provide clear visual messages to guide the learner through navigation.
- Make sure labels are clear and understandable.
- Be appropriate to the site's purpose.
- Support user's goals and behavior.

Reflection

Before closing this chapter, it is important to remind the reader that responding to students' demands is the key to successful site architecture. Here are some major concerns of students who would be using your site. Consider the following questions before, during, and after developing an e-learning site.

Students have the following general concerns when they are using e-learning sites:

- Where am I?
- Where can I go?
- How will I get there?
- How can I get back?

Students have the following concerns about the purpose of the site they are using:

- How do I begin?
- Do I need special knowledge or tools?
- How do I get information that is right for me?
- How can I try it for myself?
- What if I want to learn more?
- What if I have a question?

In e-learning, students are concerned about being assessed. They may have the following questions when they get confused:

- How do I know if I am saying the correct answer?

- What if I come across something I do not know?
- How can I try it out myself?

Part III
Orientation to Design and Development

There is extensive literature on the text based instructional design and development process (Knirk & Gustafson, 1986 and Gagne`, Briggs & Wager, 1992). The stages of instructional design and development that are most common among traditional text based approaches are needs assessment, design process, develop and implement, and evaluation and revision.

In recent years, a few attempts have been made to apply traditional instructional design and development models to the design process of the Web (Lee and Owens, 2000; Alessi and Trollip, 2001). Figure III. 1 shows a systematic model for the instructional design and development process for e-learning that underlies the present textbook.

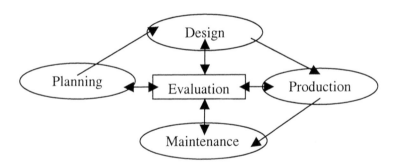

Figure III.1 Phases of Instructional Design and Development

The model presented in Figure III.1 has been adopted from the Web design guidelines that IBM has proposed. The process of design and development for e-learning in this book is similar to the model proposed by IBM. There are some modifications to the IBM model to make it more suitable for e-learning. Some of the modifications are from a text based instructional design and development process, and others are based on the author's personal experiences. The purpose of Part III is to discuss the modifications that have been added to the IBM model.

Chapter 10
The Design Process

The most successful and effective e-learning sites are those that serve students well by providing curriculum that satisfies the learners' needs in terms of content organization and presentation design. IBM has provided wonderful guidelines for the process of designing Web sites that are based on years of experience, user studies, and published books. Their guidelines for the process of designing Web sites include four phases that are planning, design, production and maintenance. The phases of the design process recommended by IBM are also ideal for developing successful and effective e-learning sites. The purpose of this chapter is to discuss the four phases of the process of Web site design as they relate to e-learning. It should be noted that these four phases recommended by IBM are slightly modified to fit the needs of the e-learning deign process.

- Planning
  - Learner Analysis: Who Will Use It?
  - Educational Goal Analysis: Determining Site's Goal
  - Identify Content
  - Task Analysis: Charting Content
  - Team Analysis: Who Will Be Involved in Development?
- Design
  - Site Architecture
  - Page Layout and Visual Design
  - Schedule of Time and Resources
- Production
  - Development
  - Final Testing
- Maintenance
  - Administration
  - Marketing Your Site

Planning
    The information gained through the analysis of the steps in the design phase will provide valuable information that will guide the educational designer through the development of an e-learning site. Without the accurate knowledge gained from these five steps in the design phase, the organization of the e-learning environment will not serve the students well.

Learner Analysis: Who Will Use It?
    Students' needs analysis is critical to designing an effective e-learning environment. With students' needs and characteristics established, you can thoughtfully structure the site to reflect their personal needs. There are two types of information (general and specific) that we need in order to make logical decisions about the design and development of student-centered e-learning environments. The general type of information includes:

- Age
- Academic level
- Sex
- Family status
- Ethnicity
- Religion
- Level of computer/internet experience
- Access to technology from home and school

    More specific information is about the personalized needs of the students' social characteristics, communication styles, personality, cognitive ability, linguistic style, and academic background. These personal attributes are gained through developmental periods, and they form children's inner perception about themselves and the world in which they live. One of the main objections to curriculum personalization is that it is impossible to personalize education for all students because there are too many unique characteristics. The issue of the infinite characteristics of all students can be considered from the psychological perspective of the most common traits within groups (Gardener, 1980). Therefore, curriculum personalization concepts discussed in this chapter are based on common group personality rather than purely individual personality. Learning about the personalized needs of the students involves: 1) becoming involved, 2) seeking appropriate information about your students, 3) determining their learning styles, and 4) recognizing design implications from your findings.

First, in order to find information about students' backgrounds requires becoming involved and seeking information from the community. There are numerous communities such as the church, workplace, art shows, ethnic festivals, social groups, support groups, and social services where information can be gathered. Furthermore, you can read magazines and focus journals about specific groups to become acquainted with their patterns of thought and their preferences. Then, you should create surveys and interviews to gain information about your students' social characteristics, communication styles, personality, cognitive ability, linguistic style, and academic background.

Second, in seeking appropriate information about your students, you should interview community members about the group dimensions, and plan the design of your e-learning site accordingly. For example, Shade, et al. (1997) have provided the following guidelines for African-American and Mexican-American cultural characteristics that contribute to the design of classrooms (Table 10.1). Similar information as that provided in Table 10.1 can help the design of e-learning in terms of visual design, site architecture, and content presentation.

(Table 10.1) Cultural Characteristics (Shade, et al., 1997)

African American Cultural Style	Mexican American Cultural Style
aesthetic appreciation of bright colors, fashionable clothing, and hair styles as the need to express their self-identity	individuals should identify closely with their community, family, and ethnic group
a deep respect for spirituality and humanness that is often manifested through religion	individuals should be very sensitive to the feelings of others
a spontaneity and ability for improvisation and rhythmic orientations shown in dance, music, and verbal and non verbal communication	status and role definitions within the community and family are clearly defined and should be respected
value system that incorporates not only the desire for success, but also group unity, freedom and equality	achievement or success is highly dependent on the cooperative efforts of individuals rather than competitive individualism.

Third, determining students' learning styles in e-learning sites has virtually been nonexistent. Even in traditional lecture-based educational settings, content has been concerned with a single learning style that assumes the human ability to learn comes out of a uniform cognitive capacity. As I mentioned in Chapter One, Howard Gardener (1983) challenged the commonly held belief of a uniform cognitive capacity for all humans by hypothesizing that human beings are capable of at least seven basic intelligences. In his book <u>Frames of Mind</u> (Gardner, 1983), Dr. Gardner seriously questioned the validity of determining a child's single intelligence away from a natural setting. Instead he proposed that intelligence has more to do with multiple cognitive capacities.

Based on his extensive research, Gardener (1983) then divided human intelligence into seven distinct yet related categories. In 1996 he added one additional intelligence to his original seven categories. The following is a brief description of his eight intelligences along with the most suitable teaching approach for an individual with different intelligences. I have also included the name of a famous character in different fields that I believe is an exemplary representative of each intelligence.

Verbal-Linguistic Intelligence: The learner manifests an extraordinary capacity to use language. This learner is good at reading, writing, story telling, and remembering names, places, and dates. The most suitable environment for these learners to learn is to provide them with the opportunity of a structured learning environment to speak, read, or write (Emily Dickinson).

Logical-Mathematical Intelligence: This type of learner likes to solve problems by hypothesizing, by asking questions, gathering patterns of information, exploring, and experimenting to find an answer to their hypotheses. This learner has a capacity to use math and logic/problem solving. Logical-mathematical learners are at the peak of their potential to learn new concepts when they are allowed to explore, gather information, and test their hypothesis (Albert Einstein).

Spatial Intelligence: This learner has the capacity to draw, design, and visualize. This person is especially proficient at imagining, sensing details, doing puzzles, and converting words into charts and maps. Spatially intelligent people absorb information by visualizing and manipulating with pictures and colors (Frank Lloyd Wright).

Musical Intelligence: This type of learner probably has the ability to produce melody and rhythms. They always listen to different music and have exceptional ability to remember patterns of music. Musically intelligent people learn best by all types of nonverbal sound, rhythms, or musical notation (John Lennon).

Bodily-Kinesthetic Intelligence: This type of learner is aware and has control of his/her physical body. They use their body to express ideas. Their tactile sense is well developed and they enjoy physical challenges. They learn best by doing, moving and being physically involved (Venus Williams).

Interpersonal Intelligence: The social butterfly. They work well within a group. Leadership is their best quality, and they know how to work well with others. Impart new information to this person by allowing cooperation with others to solve problems (Martin Luther King Jr.).

Intrapersonal Intelligence: This type of learner enjoys working alone. They follow instincts with confidence, and they are creative. They are in touch with their inner feelings and are able to set realistic goals in life. They learn best when self-paced and singularly oriented (Marie Curie).

Naturalist Intelligence: In addition to the original seven intelligences, Gardener's research revealed an eighth intelligence that he called Naturalist Intelligence. This intelligence is found in learners who love the natural world of plants and animals. This type of learner has the capacity to learn at his/her potential when natural categories of objects and living things are presented to them (Charles Darwin).

Identification of intelligences has come to be a routine task. There are some reliable batteries of diagnostic tests that determine the strong intelligences in different individuals. For example, The Multiple Intelligence Indicator developed by Silver, Strong, and Associates (1998) is one of the more reliable diagnostic tools for identifying intelligence profiles of different adult learners. Once the learner's strong intelligence is identified, then appropriate teaching models (instructional techniques) must be aligned with that particular intelligence.

It is important to mention that Gardener (1983) emphasized that people posses all these intelligences, and they use them in different situations. However, most people demonstrated exceptional ability in one or two intelligences. From an instructional point of view, it is essential to determine the intelligences that are strongest in different learners. Once these strong intelligences are identified, they can then be integrated into teaching models; and, thus, provide different presentations and organization of the same instructional materials to different learners.

Finally, during the students' needs analysis step you should recognize the design implications from your findings about the students. This type of information forms the building blocks of student-centered Web sites. Based on the profiles of the students, you should consider the following questions to prepare for the next design phase:

- Which interface design features will represent the students' multiple intelligences?
- Which instructional model should be implemented for different learning styles?
- How should the information be structured?
- How should students communicate?
- What activities should be included?
- What level of interactivity is needed?
- What linguistic style is appropriate?
- What kinds of graphics are appropriate?
- What kinds of media best represent the students' backgrounds?

Educational Goal Analysis: Determining Site's Goal

Educational goal analysis refers to the general instructional goal, or the educational problem that the e-learning environment intends to solve. Without clear identification of the educational goal, there is a good chance that the project will go astray and in many instances will fail. According to Knirk and Gustafson (1986) there are two simple stages in a systematic approach to instructional goal analysis: determine what is, what is desired, and documentation.

The first step to determine the instructional goal is the process of understanding the current educational situation (What is?) and defining the desired goal (What is desired?). The gap between the two states, what is and what is desired, defines the instructional goal for e-learning environments. For example, if the average math level of a seventh grader is pre-algebra, and the goal is to teach algebraic equations, this discrepancy between the two levels provides the educational problem that needs to be solved by the development of an e-learning environment. Once the educational goal of an e-learning environment has been determined, the producer has an excellent idea in how to plan for a site that will serve the needs of the students.

Figure 10.1 shows clarity of an academic goal. Its purpose is instantly discernible which is to provide information about *How Things Fly*. Therefore, in determining the site's goal the developer has carefully considered the following:

- The current situation (lack of knowledge about flying).
- The desired situation (knowledge about flying).
- The discrepancy between what is and what is desired (a unit on *How things Fly*).
-

Therefore, the educational goal of this site is to develop a unit on *How Things Fly*.

Figure 10.1 Clarity of Educational Goal for How Things Fly
http://www.aero.hq.nasa.gov/edu/

Defining an instructional goal for e-learning is not limited to academic disciplines or teaching. There may be many different kinds of educational purposes; for example, currently there are numerous Web sites or CD-ROMs that provide educational resources, research tools, development tools, and many other instructional supports. In these cases, it is still essential to define the current situation and the desired goal although the goal is generally much broader than academic goals. The following are examples of non-teaching goals:

- Provide educational resources on (e.g. science)
- Raise money for school
- Enhance my lectures
- Create an educational community
- Fulfill class assignments
- Complete homework

Once the gap between the two states of the current level and the desired educational goal has been determined, a clear written statement must be prepared and shared with all those involved. Sharing of the written statement can be documented and discussed in a meeting or posted on the Web to solicit responses from those people who are involved in the development.

Documentation also includes gathering a set of marketing survey results. The purpose of marketing surveys is to gain knowledge about the students' unique demography, their browser usage, their attitudes, and their preferences. Marketing surveys may also provide information about other similar sites that you intend to develop. This type of information is very useful in two ways. First, surveying other Web sites that are similar to the one you wish to develop provides information about what you may or may not want to include in your site. Second, there may be instances where your potential Web site has already been developed. In this case you would be wasting time and effort because your site may prove to be redundant.

There are some online sites that provide marketing survey results. For example, GVU WWW provides user Surveys: http://www.cc.gatech.edu/gvu/user_surveys/. To find similar Web sites, one can do a search on one of many search sites such as Netscape (http://home.netscape.com/) or Yahoo (http://www.yahoo.com/).

Identify Content

The information gathered about the learner analysis and educational goal analysis clearly provides guidance to the type of content that your e-learning site will be presenting. The content area for students may range in the elementary, middle, high school, or college level. The content area may include typical curricula that are presented in these levels of schooling. Here the expertise of teachers, professors, books, journals, Web sites and other professionals is essential. For example, if the user analysis and the educational goal analysis have determined that the content should include teaching for pre-algebra to solve algebraic equations, then the content will be provided by the expertise of a math teacher, university professor of mathematics, state level standards (such as California Standards for Mathematics), national level standards (such as The National Council of Teachers of Mathematics, NTCM), Web sites, and mathematical books related to middle school algebra. Identification of these resources and gaining legal right to use these contents become essential for the next step in the planning phase.

Identifying content for e-learning sites is not limited to academic disciplines. Content may relate to a non-instructional site spell check, educational resources, or others. For example if the educational goal of a site is to teach how to fly, then the content area needs training procedures for such a purpose. As before, the expertise of teachers who teach flying, knowledge of aeronautic professors, resources from such agencies as NASA, books, and manuals would become key to creating an effective e-learning site for learning or teaching how to fly.

Task Analysis: Charting Content

Once the learners' analysis and the educational goal of the e-learning environment have been documented, and alternative resources for content have been examined, one should perform a learning task analysis to more accurately define the steps that are needed to accomplish the main goal. Task analysis includes:

- Breakdown of the main goal into subordinating goals.
- Breakdown of the events of instruction for each subordinating goal.

Figure 10.2 illustrates a breakdown of the main goal into subordinating goals. The main goal of the *Gate-to-Gate* CD-ROM, developed by NASA is to take students behind the scenes to look at the people and the tools used to manage air traffic. The main goal has been divided into eight subordinating goals. There are seven buttons, (illustrated as jets) that the user can click on to get information about the subordinating goals. These subordinating goals were determined by the common flight profile of a commercial jetliner. This flight profile includes the following phases during a commercial jetliner's typical flight: Preflight, Take off, Departure, En Route, Descent, Approach, and Landing. Each one of these subordinating goals has been divided into five activities (events of instruction) designed to familiarize the learner with people who work as air traffic management controllers, as well as the software tools they use to manage air traffic. These activities include Introduction, People, Tools, In Depth, and Factoid. To summarize, task analysis of the *Gate-to-Gate* CD-ROM includes:

- Main goal: Illustrate the tools for air traffic management.
- Subordinating goals are: Preflight, Take-off, Departure, En Route, Descent, Approach, and Landing.
- Events of instruction for each subordinating goal: Introduction, People, Tools, In Depth, and Factoid.

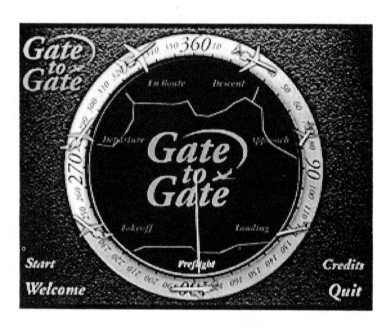

Figure 10.2 Initial Screen Shot of Gate-to-Gate CD-ROM

It is difficult to show all the subordinating goals and their activities in the screen shot of the *Gate-to-Gate* CD-ROM. The most convenient way for developers to visualize these subordinating goals and their activities is to use a flowchart. Figure 10.3 illustrates the flowchart for the *Gate-to-Gate* CD-ROM. The tree hierarchy that is created clearly shows the flow of subordinating goals and their activities. There are seven subordinating goals as indicated by Preflight, Take off, etc. These subordinating goals are represented by buttons shaped as jetliners on the CD-ROM main interface. With the exception of the Start (Introduction) to the CD-ROM and the Quit button, each subordinating goal has five events of instruction that include Introduction, People, Tools, In-Depth, and Factoids.

This type of flowcharting of the activities of a multimedia-learning environment allows modification and revision before the actual CD-ROM is developed. Flowcharting saves a tremendous amount of money, development time, and manpower. Once the flowchart is revised, the design and organization of content (site architecture) will become easier and more effective.

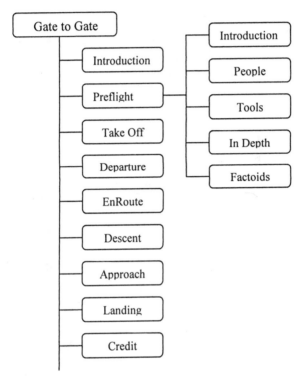

Figure 10.3 Flowchart for Gate-to-Gate CD-ROM

Events of instruction are sometimes much more complicated than is shown in the flowchart of Figure 10.3. For example, if one of the subordinating goals of a multimedia-learning environment is to teach solving equations, the events of instruction must first be determined. Instructional designers visualize complex events of instruction in a flowchart. Figure 10.4 describes a simple flowchart of the events of instruction that are needed for solving equations with two variables. Once again, flowcharting simplifies the process of development and allows revision before the actual production is initiated.

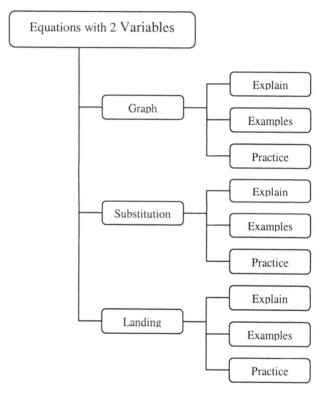

Figure 10.4 Flowchart of Events of Instruction for
Equations with Two Variables

Team Analysis: Who Will Be Involved in Development?

A team approach to producing an e-learning environment is strongly recommended. Depending on the nature of the project, team members involved vary from project to project. There are two kinds of members in a team: the core members and the supporting members. The core members include a project manager, a programmer, and a subject matter expert. The supporting members may include an audio producer, video producer, media specialist, graphic artist, editor, instructional designer, secretarial support, and a scriptwriter. In a larger scale educational multimedia-learning environment, there may be a need for actors/actresses, a narrator, a personal assistant and other more specialized personnel.

The supporting team members as well as the core members should have the following characteristics for the success of the project.

- Social skills: Creating a multimedia-learning environment is an intense endeavor. Team members must have the ability to respect other members and be socially responsible under pressure.
- Communication skills: The ability to effectively communicate with the other members is crucial to the success of a project
- Flexibility: Team members must be flexible and assume new roles if it becomes necessary.
- Creativity: Multimedia-learning environments are such a new medium for teaching that the creativity of the individuals involved will make the project stand out.
- Ability to accept criticism: Constructive criticism is a key to the success of a project. Throughout the project the team must evaluate their production and be ready to accept criticism. Any educational project must have continuous evaluation and revision throughout the production as well as in postproduction.
- Commitment to the goal of the project: Individuals should not have their own goal for the project. It must be made very clear that all team members must commit to the goal of the project.

Furthermore, after a team has been selected, specific relationship guidelines must be established for everyone to follow. These guidelines may include:

- Positive inter-group relationship.
- Respectful and equal treatment for all team members.

- Careful listening of other's opinion.
- Mistakes by members should not be criticized, but be considered as a source of learning.
- Members should clearly communicate their progress. Members should not assume, but listen to what has been communicated.
- Sharing progress with all members of the team should be encouraged.

In addition to the attributes mentioned for team members, the team leader who is generally the project manager should have the following characteristics to be an effective leader:

- Sharing of responsibility is a source of power.
- Should not be threatened by team member's ability in specific professional skill.
- Should place emphasis on team approach throughout the entire production.
- Must recognize effective team functions.

It is important to mention that one of the most essential team members during production, who is often ignored, is the student pilot. The student pilot is a typical student who will be using the multimedia-learning environment. Every attempt must be met to ensure that at least one student representing the target audience is involved in the project. The role of the student pilot will be both as an advisor as well as an evaluator of the outcome of the project. This does not mean that the team will be asking the student about how to design a unit. Rather his advising is mirrored in the process of development. Evaluation of an e-learning site takes place by asking the student pilot to actually use the site. Depending on his reaction as well as his learning outcome, the team members, especially the instructional designer, can evaluate the effectiveness of the Web site.

Design
     The design issues are concerned with the site architecture, navigation, page layout, visual design, and schedule of time and resources.

Site Architecture
     The site architecture of an e-learning site should be easy to use for the learner, and more important it should be based on the way the developer wishes to organize the site based on the learners' learning styles as well as the type of content that the site will present. In Chapter 9, I presented a variety of site architecture including single page architecture, sequential architecture, hierarchical architecture, grid architecture, and network architecture. Each of these site architectures may serve different leaning styles, the task analysis, and content flowcharting. Below, find some guidelines that will help you to address your choice of the type of site architecture that would satisfy the goal(s) of your e-learning site:

- Use single page architecture when the needs of your students and the structure of content dictate limiting the learner's control because there are no external links.
- Use a forward sequential site architecture when your content and the needs of the learner's learning style require focusing on the same topic in a specific order.
- Use two-way sequential site architecture when your site requires that students should learn cause and effect. This type of site architecture allows learners to go back and forth when they need to see the cause or re-examine the effect.
- When your content organization requires additional detailed information for a given topic, use sequential site architecture with an optional two-way path. Such a structure allows learners to get further information when they need it and to return to the original topic. If the

learner does not require the additional information, they can just skip the path and go to the next topic.

- Use grid site architecture when your content compares and contrasts topics. For example, a lesson on the history of the American Revolution can be presented in a grid-like structure. Each column represents one perspective of the same event. The first column may be information about the American Revolution from the perspective of the U.S. The second column may be information about the American Revolution from a British point of view and so on. Students compare and contrast the historical events from different perspectives.

- When your content organization or your students learning styles require categories and subcategories or classification, use hierarchical site architecture. In such an organization the main topic is divided into several subtopics. Each of the subtopics provides the second layer of the hierarchy. If the subtopic needs further classification, then the new subtopic becomes the third layer of the hierarchy.

- Use network architecture when your content or the learning styles of students require discovery through association. Such exploration generally allows navigation under the control of the learner.

Page Layout and Visual Design

Using your user's analysis, the flowchart of your content, and the information about visual design provided in Chapters 6 and 9 of this book, decide what type of visual design will most likely appeal to your students. It is really important to use the type of information provided in this chapter (see Table 10.1) to personalize the visual design for your users. For example, an e-learning site whose audience is mostly Hispanic, will prefer certain colors and artifacts that other cultures may not find appealing.

Once you have decided on the design and the arrangements of the elements of design such as text, graphics, color, media, etc., it is really useful to obtain index cards and sketch the visual layout and visual design that reflect the preference of your user. These index cards can then be arranged according to the flowchart of content representing the site architecture that you had prepared previously. Before any coding is done to actually develop your e-learning site, consider asking several of your pilot students to look at the index cards and their arrangements. After soliciting feedback from your users and other members of your development team, revise the sketches and their arrangement. Such revisions are most helpful before any coding is done because it saves time, energy and resources. It is also important to keep the following guidelines in mind before actual coding begins:

- Be consistent in your visual design and page layouts.
- Present information efficiently and take advantage of white space.
- Use of alignment for text and graphics allows users to scan your pages easier.
- Avoid asking the users to scroll horizontally or vertically to find more information.
- Use the top of each page for displaying logos and titles.
- Use the left side of pages for menus or navigational systems.
- Use the right side of each page for content presentation.
- Avoid using the bottom of pages for menu or navigational systems.

Production

Production refers to applying all the planning that you have done to actually programming the codes that are necessary for the e-learning site to be functional. Such a process includes production of HTML codes, preparation of text, images, audio, video, and other elements of design. What makes e-learning sites different from other Web sites in the process of production is the development of supporting curricula materials such as manuals, tests, learning guides, directions, answers to questions, grading, etc. Some of these materials may require a traditional text or video based approach. During development it is really important to follow a continuous evaluation process from pilot students as well as other local, state, and national users.

To produce an e-learning site that is effective, one must follow a team approach. In many cases, an individual assumes all the roles and attempts to produce an e-learning site by himself/herself. This approach is not advisable. If an e-learning site is to be effective, it requires the collaboration of many experts. As mentioned before, a team may include core experts such as a programmer, interface designers, or an instructional designer and supportive members such as writers, an audio and video producer, and others. In short, for an e-learning site to be professional so that it would satisfy the needs of the students, a team approach is the way to go.

Development
The actual production requires the following steps:

- Study the paper and pencil design.
- Programmers, designers, and content developer must review the flowchart and the paper and pencil design.
- Determine which authoring tool or programming language must be used.
- Determine browser compatibility.
- Produce first module.
- Review and revise the first module.
- Produce the remaining module.
- Evaluation
- Revise at all levels of storyboards, flowcharts, and development.

Final Testing
In most cases, e-learning sites are first developed on the desktop of a workstation. As the last revision has been performed for all modules, move all the folders and directories onto a Web server. This will give you better testing results as the

users actually use the site from a server. Most users still use a 28.8 modem. Make sure the first page will be loaded within the first 10 seconds. It is very difficult to keep the learners attention if the site is slow to load. It is also critical to test how different browsers function at this stage. This is because the appearance of all the elements of design such as color, text, images, video, and audio depends on the type of browser and the operating system the learner is using. The best testing results are gained if you test all pages of your e-learning site using different browsers and different operating systems.

Maintenance
The purpose of maintenance is administration and marketing your site.

Administration
It is important to have a competent administrator who is aware of Web technologies to administrate the e-learning site. The administrator will make certain that the site is continuously updated both in terms of content as well as the result of evaluation of the site. Based on the evaluation, the administrator should make sure that the links are working properly, the images are compatible with the color schemes of different browsers, the media load fast, and the administrator should track the learners activities. If the e-learning site has chat rooms or forums, the administrator should make sure that these rooms are monitored and well maintained. Most important the administrator should respond to the feedback from the learner and implement appropriate changes to satisfy the needs of the learners.

Marketing Your Site
IBM recommends the following key issues to market your site:

- Place keywords in the meta information.
- Announce your site on relevant news groups and bulletin boards.

- Advertise on major sites.
- Advertise through other media such as magazines, radio and television.

Reflections

The goal of this book has been to discuss the design of e-learning sites from a perceptual design and content organization. Perceptual design, as we have seen in this book, is about how an e-learning site can visually communicate ease of use by using techniques that visual designers employ from the fields of interface design, site architecture, and page layout sources. The content organization is about how an e-learning site can organize its content according to educational psychology theories. The most effective way to see if an e-learning site has successfully implemented the issues that I have covered in this book is to follow a systematic evaluation process that includes a feedback process. Therefore, a successful evaluation of an e-learning site should cover three levels of evaluation that include feedback level, content organization, and the perceptual level.

Feedback Level

The feedback level should use the same mechanism as traditional evaluation of training programs. In traditional university courses, instructors as well as the content and organization of the course is evaluated when the course is completed.   E-learning sites should also follow the same procedure except it should be an electronic version rather than the written traditional form. Furthermore, evaluation should not be limited to the end of the course. There should also be some form of evaluation during the time students are completing the course. The electronic forms of the evaluation after completion of the course can be in the form of questionnaires, chat rooms, discussion in forum, email, etc.

It is best to make questionnaires in a simple multiple-choice format so that learners can just click their choice. Such choices could be on a Likert-scale from 1 to 5 where 1 is strongly disagree and 5 is strongly agree. Of course the adjectives describing the levels of the Likert-scale would change depending on the question. Such a scale would make it easier for a database to evaluate the results regardless of the adjectives that are used.

Online discussion such as a chat room or forum would allow other participants to read the view of others. This may provide the foundation for creating focus groups where students can collectively provide feedback to the developer of the e-learning site. Email is also a very effective way of getting feedback from the students. These types of electronic tools can be used both during the time that the students are using the e-learning environment as well as when the course is completed.

Content Organization

The evaluation of the content organization is concerned with whether the educational goal(s) of the e-learning site has been achieved. This level of evaluation focuses on the way the educational materials have been organized. If you recall from Part I of this book, the organization of materials is based on learning theories. However, such theories should be transparent to the learner. We simply can not ask the learner whether Piaget's concept of learning and the teaching model derived from it have been effective or not. Rather, measurement of the effectiveness of an e-learning site must rely on the achievement of the students. If the goals of the site have been achieved, that simply means the theoretical foundation of the site was also appropriate.

A non-electronic course measures learning either through written quizzes, midterms or final exams. Fortunately, the electronic evaluation for learning can assume many different versions rather than the more conventional written version. The simplest and easiest way to measure achievement of an e-learning site is to design an electronic test based on conventional methods that rely on the following techniques: true/false, multiple choice, matching list, fill-in-blank, or text input.

Fortunately, evaluation of learning using technology allows much more effective and interesting approaches. Using the capabilities of technology, you can design activities to measure the achievements of your students. Some of these techniques include simulation, hands-on activities, online role playing, electronic games, and live questions and answers using messaging or chat rooms.

In addition to evaluating the e-learning site in terms of achievement of its educational goal(s), there are some concerns about the instructional design issues of the site. The following questions may be designed with online responses based on a Likert-scale to ask learners to clarify some of these issues:

- Was the site educationally beneficial to you?
- Was sequence of instruction logical?
- Is the material relevant to the objects of the site?
- Did you know how to get started and what to do?
- Did the site content provide adequate information?
- Did the site have any errors in terms of facts or figures?
- Did the site deliver the type of site (e.g. simulation, tutorial) it promised?
- Did the testing or evaluation reflect the content of the course?

Perceptual Level

The perceptual level is concerned with three aspects of design that include the interface, site architecture, and the navigational system. To measure the effectiveness of the perceptual level, it is best to make questionnaires in a simple multiple-choice format so that the learners can just click their choice. (Such choices could be on a Likert-scale from 1 to 5 where 1 is poor and 5 is excellent.) The following questions may be design with online responses to ask learners to evaluate the effectiveness of the elements of the perceptual level:

- Were the images relevant to the content?
- Did you like the colors on the site?
- Was the text legible and error free?
- Was the layout of the site confusing?

- Were multimedia elements such as audio or video appropriately used?
- Was the navigational system easy to use?
- Were links provided appropriately?
- Were you ever lost or not able to find your way on the site?
- Were you confused about the intentions of the icons?

Evaluation and getting feedback from the learner is not a one-time procedure. Rather, evaluation should be a continuous process where the learner is constantly involved. Each time you evaluate your site, the feedback that is provided by the learner should be shared with all the team members who helped develop the site. After sharing or discussing the relevancy of the feedback, appropriate revision must take place. The evaluation starts all over again and revision is made. Such a continuous process will make the e-learning site student centered and satisfy the educational needs of the learner.

Bibliography

Alvarez, Richard, Taylor, Jason & Groch, Matthew. (2002) *Generator/Flash Web development* (With CD-ROM). Indianapolis: New Rider.

Anderson, R. A., & Pearson, P. D. (1984). A schema-theoretic view of basis processes in reading comprehension. In P. D. Pearson (Ed.), *Handbook of reading research* (pp. 255-292). New York: Longmans.

Apple, Michael. (1990). *Ideology and curriculum.* New York: Routledge.

Appleberry, James, B. (1992). "Changes in our future: how will we cope?" Faculty speech presented at the California State University, Long Beach, California

Ausubel, D. P. (1968). *Education psychology: A cognitive view.* New York: Holt, Rinehart & Winston.

Bock, P. K. (1988). *Rethinking psychological anthropology: Continuity and change in the study of human action.* New York: W.H. Freeman.

Bransford, J., Brown, Ann L., and Cocking, Rodney, R. (1999). *How people learn: Brain, mind, experience, and school.* Washington D.C. National academy Press.

Brumbaugh-Duncan, Cheryl. (2002) *The Flash MX project.* Indianapolis : New Riders

Bruner, J. (1960). *The process of education.* Cambridge, MA: Harvard University Press.

Bruner, J. (1966). *Toward a theory of instruction.* Cambridge, MA: Harvard University Press.

Burger, Jeff. (1994). *The desktop multimedia bible.* Menlo Park California: Addison-Wesley Publishing Company.

Capra, Fritjof . (1996). *The web of life: a new scientific understanding of living systems.* New York: Anchor Books,

Carroll J. B. (1963). A model of school learning. Teacher College Record, 64, 723-733.

Chi, M.T.H., Glaser, R., & Rees, E. (1982). *Expertise in problem solving.* In R.J. Sternberg (Ed.), *Advances in the psychology of human intelligence: Vol. 1.* Hillsdale, N.J.: Erlbaum.

Chun, Russell. (2002) *Macromedia Flash MX advanced for Windows and Macintosh visual QuickPro guide.* Berkeley: Macromedia Press.

Collins, A., Brown, J. S., & Newman, S. E. (1989). Cognitive apprenticeship: Teaching the crafts of reading, writing, and mathematics. In L. B. Resnick (Ed.), *Knowing, learning, and instruction: Essays in honor of Robert Glaser* (pp. 453-494). Hillsdale, NJ: Lawrence Erlbaum Associates.

CTGV (Cognition and Technology Group at Vanderbilt University). (1993). Designing learning environments that support thinking: Jasper series as a case study. In T.M. Duffy, J. Lowyck, D. H. Jonassen and T.M. Welsh (eds) *Designing Environments for constructive Learning,* New York: Springer-Verlag.

CTGV (Cognition and Technology Group, Learning Technology Center, Peabody College of Vanderbilt University). (1991). Technology and the design of generative learning environments, Education Technology, 31, (5), 34-40.

Dick, W., & Carey, L. (1990). *The systematic design of instruction,* (3rd ed.). Glenville, IL: Harper-Collins.

Elvin, L. (1977). *The place of common sense in educational thought.* London: Unwin Educational Books.

England, E., & Finney, A. (1996) *Managing multimedia.* New York: Addison.

Erikson, Erik H. (1950). *Childhood and society.* New York: W.W. Norton.

Flavell, J. H. (1985). *Cognitive development* (2nd ed.) Englewood Cliffs, NJ: Prentice-Hall.

Freud, Anna. (1946). *The ego and the mechanism of defense.* New York: International Universities Press.

Gagne, R. M., Briggs, L. L., & Wager, W. W. (1992). *Principles of instructional design* (4th ed.). New York: Harcourt Brace Jovanovich.

Gardner, H. (1983). *Frames of mind: The theory of multiple intelligences.* New York: Basic Books.

Gillani, B.B. (1994). *Application of Vygotsky's social cognitive theory to the design of instructional materials.* Unpublished doctoral dissertation, University of Southern California.

Gillani, B. B. (1998). The web as a delivery medium to enhance instruction. *Journal of Educational Media International.* (pp. 35 (3) 197-202.

Gillani, B. B. & A. Relan (1997). Incorporating interactivity and multimedia into web-based instruction: In B. Khan (ed.) *Web-based instruction* (pp. 231-239). Englewood Cliffs: Educational Technology Publication.

Horton, William (1994). *Designing and writing online documentation.* New York: John Wiley & Sons, Inc.

Horton, William (1994). *The icon book: Visual symbols for computer systems and documentation.* New York: John Wiley & Sons, Inc

IBM, http://www.ibm.com/easy

Jacobson, Dov & Jacobson, Jesse. (2001) *Flash and XML: A Developer's guide.* Boston: Addison-Wesley.

Jonassen, D. (1991, September). Evaluating constructive learning. *Educational Technology*, 32, 28-33.

Kay, Allen (2001). User interface: A personal view. In Packer R., and Ken Jordan (Eds.) *Multimedia* (pp. 121-131). New York. W.W.Norton & Company.

Kerman, Phillip. (2002) *ActionScripting in Flash MX.* Indianapolis: New Rider.

Knirk, F.G. & Gustafson, Kent. (1986). *Instructional technology: A system approach to education.* San Francisco: Holt, Rinehart and Winston, Inc.

Kovalik, S. (1994). *Integrated thematic instruction: The model.* Kent, WA: Susan Kovalick.

Larkin, J., McDermott, J., Simon, D.P., & Simon, H.A. (1980). Expert and novice performance in solving physics problems. Science, 208, 1335-1342.

Laurillard, D. (1993). *Rethinking university teaching: A framework for effective use of educational technology.* New York: Routledge.

Lee and Owens, and Alessi and Trollip. (2001). *Multimedia for learning: Methods and development.*Boston: Allyn and Bacon.

Moock, Colin & Grossman, Gary (2002) ActionScript : The definitive guide. Cambridge: O'Reilly.

Mullet, Kevin, & Sano, Darrel. (1995). *Designing visual interfaces.* Mountain View, CA: SunSoft Press.

Norman, Donald. (1988). *The design of everyday things.* New York: Doubleday.

O'Keefe, J., & Nadel, L. (1978). *The hippocampus as a cognitive map.* Oxford: Clarendon Press.

Papert, S. (1993). *The children's machine.* New York: Basic Books.

Papert, S. (1980). *Mindstorms: children, computers and powerful Ideas.* New York: Basic Books.

Piaget, J. (1926). *The language and thought of the child.* New York: Harcourt Brace Jovanovich.

Piaget, J. (1952). *The origins of intelligence in children.* New York: International Universities Press.

Piaget, J. (1964). Development and learning. In R. E. Ripple & V. N. Rockcastle (Eds.), *Piaget rediscovered: A report of the conference on cognitive skills and curriculum development.* Ithaca, NY: Cornell University, School of Education.

Rosebush, J.(1995). A guide to multimedia production staff. CD-ROM Professional, 8(7), 32-43.

Sahlin, Doug (2002) *Macromedia Flash(R) MX virtual classroom.* New York: McGraw Hill

Sanders, Bill. (2001). Flash actionScript f/x and design. Scottsdale: Coriolis.

Schniederman, Ben. (1998). *Designing the user interface: strategies for effective human-computer interaction.* Berkeley, California: Addison-Wesley.

Senge, Peter M. (1990). *The fifth discipline: the art and practice of the learning organization.* New York: Currency Doubleday.

Shade, B.J., Kelly, C., & Oberg, M. (1997). *Creating culturally responsive classrooms.* Washington D.C.: American Psychological Association.

Skinner, B.F. (1953). *Science and human behavior.* New York: Macmillan.

Skinner, B.F. (1954). The science of learning and the art of teaching. *Harvard Educational Review.* 24, 86-97.

Skinner, B.F. (1986). Programmed instruction revisited. Phi Delta Kappan, 68, 103-110.

Suppes, P. (1969). Computer technology and the future of education. In Atkinson and H.A. Wilson (eds.), *Computer-assisted instruction.: A book of readings..* New York: Academic Press.

Suppes, P. (1980). Impact of computers on curriculum in schools and universities." In Taylor, R (ed). *The computers in the school: Tutor, tool, tutee.* New York: Teacher College Press. 236-247.

Thorndike, E.L. (1913). *Education psychology.* New York: Columbia University, Teacher College Press.

Thrap and Gallimore (1992). *Rousing minds to life: Teaching, learning, and schooling in social context.* Victoria, Australia. Cambridge University Press.

Toffler, Alvin. (1970). *Future Shock.* New York: Bantam Books.

Turner, Bill, Robertson, James & Richard Bazley. (2001). *Flash 5 cartoons and games f/x and design.* Scottsdale: Coriolis.

Ulrich, Katherine and Russell Chun. (2002) Macromedia Flash MX for Windows and Macintosh (visual quickStart guide). Berkeley: Peachpit Press

Voss, B. A. (1982). *Summary of research in science education.* Columbus, OH: ERIC Clearinghouse for Science, Mathematics, and Environmental Education.

Vygotsky, L. S. (1962). *Thought and language* (A. Kozulin, Ed. & Trans.). Cambridge, MA: MIT Press.

Vygotsky, L. S. (1978). *Mind in society: The development of higher psychological processes* (M. Cole, V. John-Steiner, S. Scribner, & Soubermann, Eds. & Trans.). Cambridge, MA: MIT Press.

Vygotsky, L. S. (1992). *Thought and language* (A. Kozulin, Ed. & Trans.). Cambridge, MA: MIT Press.

Wurman, Saul (1989). *Information anxiety.* New York: Doubleday.

Author Biographical Sketch

Bijan Gillani received his doctorate from the University of Southern California in Curriculum and Technology. Currently he is a professor of Educational Technology in the California State University, Hayward. Professor Gillani coordinates the Graduate Program in Educational Technology Leadership and teaches courses in "Learning Theories and Educational Multimedia Design", "Web-based Instruction", "Instructional Content Development", Educational Interface Design", and "Human-Computer Interaction." He is also the Director of two grants for integration of technology into curriculum. He has been a keynote speaker and presenter at conferences on the integration of multimedia in education, e-learning, and has consulted for public and private agencies, NASA, and educational institutions. Most recently, he was the keynote speaker at the "Information Literacy" Conference, presented at the "IBM Interface Design" Conference at the IBM Research Center in New York and San Jose, and ITiRA Conference at Central Queensland University, Australia. Some of Dr. Gillani's recent publications appear in the following:

Gillani, B.B., & Relan, A. (1997). Incorporating interactivity & multimedia into web-based instruction. In B. H. Khan (Ed.), *Web-based instruction* (pp. 231-237). Englewood Cliffs, New Jersey: Educational Technology Publications.

Gillani, B.B., & Relan, A. (1997). Web-based information and the traditional classroom: similarities and differences. In B. H. Khan (Ed.), *Web-based instruction* (pp. 41-46). Englewood Cliffs, New Jersey: Educational Technology Publications.

Gillani, B.B. (1998). The web as a delivery medium to enhance instruction. *Educational Media International*, 35:3, 197-202.

Gillani, B.B. (Fall 2000). Culturally responsive educational web sites. *Educational Media International*, 37:3, 185-195.

Gillani, B.B. (2000). Student-centered design. In C. Romm & W. Taylor (Eds.), *Using community informatics for regional transformation,* (pp. 140-160). Rockhampton, Australia: University of Queensland Press.

Gillani, B.B. (2000). Using the web to create student-centered curriculum. In R.A. Cole (Ed.), *Issues in web-based pedagogy: A critical primer* (pp.161-181). Westport, Connecticut: Greenwood Press.

Gillani, B.B. (2001). Creating multiculturally responsive educational settings on the web. In L. Ramirez & O. Gallardo (Eds.), *Portraits of teachers in multicultural settings: A critical literacy approach* (pp. 123-138). Boston, Massachusetts: Allyn and Bacon.

Gillani, B.B. (2001). Educational management system. IBM Make IT Easy Conference: 2001. http://www-3.ibm.com/ibm/easy/eou_ext.nsf/Publish/1566

Gillani, B.B. (2001). Integrated learner-centered management system. In S. Marshall & W. Taylor (Eds.), *Using informatics to transform regions* (pp.451-467). Rockhampton, Australia: University of Queensland Press.

Gillani, B.B. (2002). Integrated thematic multimedia learning environments. In Stewart, Taylor, & Yu (Eds.), *Transforming regional economies and communities with information technology.* Rockhampton, Australia: University of Queensland Press.

Gillani, B.B. (2003). Integrated assessment as the basis of learner-centered design. In Stewart, Taylor, & Yu (Eds.), *Closing the digital divide.* Westport: Praeger Publishers.

Index